# Tips and Traps

## When

## Selling a Home

## Other McGraw-Hill Books by Robert Irwin

# Tips and Traps When Selling a Home

### Fourth Edition

## ROBERT IRWIN

New York   Chicago   San Francisco   Lisbon   London   Madrid   Mexico City
Milan   New Delhi   San Juan   Seoul   Singapore   Sydney   Toronto

## The *McGraw·Hill* Companies

1 2 3 4 5 6 7 8 9 0   FGR/FGR   0 1 5 4 3 2 1 0 9 8

ISBN: 978-0-07-150839-1
MHID:   0-07-150839-2

This publication is designed to provide accurate and authoritative information in regard to the subject matter covered. It is sold with the understanding that neither the author nor the publisher is engaged in rendering legal, accounting, futures/securities trading, tax, or other professional service. If legal advice or other expert assistance is required, the services of a competent professional person should be sought.

> —*From a Declaration of Principles jointly adopted*
> *by a Committee of the American Bar*
> *Association and a Committee of Publishers*

AUTHOR'S NOTE: Laws and regulations that affect the buying, selling, financing, and taxation of real estate are from time to time passed, changed, or amended by federal or state governments. Therefore, check with a real estate professional before taking action on real estate to see how this could affect you.

The term Realtor® is a registered collective membership mark that identifies a real estate professional who is a member of the National Association of Realtors®.
"MLS.com America's Real Estate Portal" is a servicemark of MLS Network, Inc.

McGraw-Hill books are available at special quantity discounts to use as premiums and sales promotions, or for use in corporate training programs. To contact a representative please visit the Contact Us pages at www.mhprofessional.com.

**Library of Congress Cataloging-in-Publication Data**

Irwin, Robert.
    Tips and traps when selling a home / by Robert Irwin.—4th ed.
        p.    cm.
    ISBN 0-07-150839-2 (alk. paper)
    1. House selling.   2. Real estate business.   I. Title.
    HD1379.I674 2009
    643.12—dc22

                                            2008027101

This book is printed on acid-free paper.

*For Amber, Joshua, and Adam*
*where the future begins*

# Contents

# 6 Steps to Selling Your Home Immediately

---

What does it take to sell your home today?

We all intuitively know that given enough time, any home will sell. Of course, it could take many months or even years. But leave it on the market long enough and you'll get your price. If for no other reason than inflation, eventually the market will catch up to whatever you're asking.

If you're reading this book, however, you probably don't have years—you're looking to sell quite a bit sooner. Maybe you'd like to sell within a month or two, perhaps within just a few weeks. Or right away?

So how do you sell in today's challenging market? How do you get a sale regardless of economic conditions?

The "how to" details are in this book, but, the quick answers are in this chapter. Here's what you need to do to sell your home in six easy-to-understand steps.

## Step 1: Compare It

Your home isn't for sale in a vacuum. You're in competition with everyone else out there. And, as you may have noticed, there are lots of other homes for sale.

**TRAP**

Don't trap yourself into thinking that no homes are selling. In the hottest market in history (2005), over 6.5 million homes were resold in the United States. But in one of the coldest markets (2008), there were still an estimated over 4 million resales. Somewhere out there, people are still buying, and lots of them selling, properties regardless of what the market looks like.

Buyers will have noticed, too. Today's buyer, if not fickle, is extremely discriminating. Today's buyer wants to be absolutely sure that he or she is not overpaying. (It hardly makes sense to pay too much if there's a buyers' market.)

This person typically begins a house hunt by checking the Internet to see what's available and at what cost. (The most widely viewed "for sale" site, Realtor.com, has well over a million listings from the Multiple Listing Service. The vast majority of buyers look there first to see what's for sale in their target area.)

**TIP**

Over 80 percent of buyers first check homes for sale on the Internet. Over 85 percent of homes are sold with the help of an agent.

Buyers also go out with agents who typically tour dozens of homes. Many thorough buyers will look at every other home for sale in the neighborhood to compare location, size, features, and, of course, price.

Thus, you must assume that by the time a buyer comes by to see your home, he or she has an excellent idea what's for sale out there and how much it should cost. Buyers quickly see where your home fits in the market.

You have to assume that today the typical buyer knows what a home such as yours, in the condition it's in, should sell for.

## Are You as Educated About the Market as Your Buyer?

Do you know as much as that buyer does? Do you know where your home fits into the market? Do you know what other homes are for sale in your price range and neighborhood?

If you want to sell, you need to know what you're up against.

Thus, learning about your competition (and comparing your home to it) should be your first step in your sales effort. Get a good CMA—and assume that every buyer will.

> **TIP**
>
> A CMA is a comparative market analysis. It takes a look at all the homes sold in your area in the past six months or so and compares them to yours. From the CMA you can quickly see how your home stacks up and, most importantly, what you can likely charge for it.

Every agent trying to list your home should be willing to prepare a free CMA for you as part of his or her presentation. It should be the agent's primary information source to help you decide on what price to ask. It will list every comparable nearby sale going back at least six months. And it will show how closely your home compares to others that have sold, in terms of square footage, bedrooms and bathrooms, location, amenities, and so forth.

Of course, you needn't rely on an agent to prepare a CMA for you. You can easily get one on your own. Many Web sites such as www.reiclub.com, www.homevalue.com, or www.homeagain.com will prepare a CMA for your house for a nominal fee, typically around $25.

Or you can prepare one yourself using a free resource such as www.zillow.com which gives you nearly all the information you'll need on recent home sales in your area.

Only after you have your CMA in hand will you clearly know what the buyers know: what your house is likely worth compared to past sales, given its location, condition, and the amenities it offers.

Getting that price figure to aim at is your first step in selling your home.

However, remember that the value of a home, like the value of a car or almost anything else, is directly related to its condition. The better the condition, the more you're likely to get for it. If you want to get top dollar for your home, you have to prep it. (For more details, check out the next section.)

## Step 2: Prep It

Preparing your home is a "must do" if you want to sell quickly and for the most money. You can think of the preparation as returning the home to the condition it was in when it was new. Of course, many sellers have improved their homes. They've added double pane windows, or a new wooden door, or stone kitchen counters, or many other highly desired features.

If you have any questions regarding what's involved in prepping your home, think of it this way: You've received a letter from the President of the United States asking you to attend a formal dinner at the White House. Of course you plan to attend. (Regardless of political preferences, this is an invitation that almost no one will turn down.)

But what will you wear?

Budgets will get thrown out the window. Tailored tuxes are in order for the men and fashionable evening gowns for the women. There's your hair to get groomed, your shoes to polish, your face to prepare, and on and on. For an occasion of this kind you simply must look your best.

Well, your house isn't likely to be visited by the President. But in terms of getting it sold, the buyer is just as important. You need it to look its best, to make the best possible impression.

TIP

"Curb appeal" gauges your house's appearance when buyers first drive up to it. That's often the split second when the "buy/don't buy" decision is made. Remember, you never get a second chance to make a good first impression.

Since you want the buyer to see your home in its best shape—not in a clean-up phase—you'll want to do the following *before* putting your home up for sale:

### 10 Things You Should Do to Prep Your House for Sale

1. **Clean.** The driveway, walkways, and the front of the house. Clean the kitchen and bathrooms. Clean the carpet and windows. Make sure that all cooking utensils are put away before showing.
2. **Paint.** The front of the house, the front door (or stain it if needed), the entryway, and all other rooms in which the paint is scratched, faded, or peeling. (And do a good job! Don't smear colors and be careful with the woodwork.)
3. **Replace.** Anything that's worn out, including torn screens, broken interior doors, switches that don't work, and any appliances that don't function properly.
4. **Garden.** Make sure your front lawn is always mowed, remove shrubs and trees that hide your home, and border it with colorful flowers.
5. **Remove the clutter.** Your home has too much furniture and clothing in it. How do I know it's there? Because all homes are that way. (Yes, you could be an exception, but are you really?) Get rid of a third of your furniture: store it, sell it, or give it away. Pull out half the clothes and

shoes from your closets: store them, give them away, or throw them out. Get rid of boxes and clean out the garage, basement, and attic.

6. **Recheck the carpet.** If a thorough cleaning didn't make it look like new. You might even consider putting in inexpensive new carpeting. Yes, this is a big expense, but it's the cheapest major thing you can do to improve the interior of your home.

7. **Stage.** Ask an agent, a friend who knows interior decorating, or hire a professional stager to come in and rearrange your furniture. You may end up moving things around and buying some new items, especially colorful covers and wraps. But your home should end up looking highly desirable, like a model home in a new housing tract.

8. **Add lighting.** Nothing detracts from a home like dark corners. The cheapest way to get rid of them is to purchase inexpensive lighting from places like Lowe's or Home Depot, use the maximum recommended wattage bulbs, and place them in all dark areas. (Just don't forget to turn them on when your house is being shown.)

9. **Clean up the back and side yards.** Debris tends to accumulate there. You needn't put in new landscaping, just mow the lawn, throw out old, damaged, or worn garden furniture, and add a few colorful flowers.

10. **Get rid of odors.** If you have pets, get rid of that old litter box, replace carpeting that they have urinated on, get rid of any moldy smells, open the windows (when possible), use air fresheners as needed, or have something yummy baking in the oven or cooking on the stove such as cookies or apple cider. And be sure the inside temperature is warm in winter and cool in summer. Nothing turns buyers off like a house that makes them sweat or freeze.

Of course, there are a host of other things you can do to shape up your home and we'll explore them in Chapter 3. But, these are the basics. If you want an immediate sale, at the least get these done. (And check out Chapter 4.)

## Step 3: Agentize It

As noted earlier, buyers use agents to find homes for them. Agents sell 85 percent of the homes in the United States. If you want to sell your home quickly and don't want to do the sales work yourself, then you should use an agent. (There's a long tradition of selling by owners in this country, and if you want to try that—and save the commission!—look into Chapter 7.)

There are three big reasons that you should consider using an agent to sell your home:

### 3 Reasons to Use an Agent

1. **Buyers prefer to work with agents.** They know that in most cases you, the seller, are paying the agent, so it won't cost them anything. Furthermore, the agent can save time. He or she can do all the legwork for them, like scouting and previewing houses to eliminate those that won't work. Finally, the agent can negotiate for them with you. Most buyers simply don't like negotiating directly with sellers. They find it too confrontational.

2. **Agents can provide you with buyers.** The MLS (Multiple Listing Service) allows all the Realtors in your area to work together on selling your home. Thus, when you sign up with an agent who is a member of the MLS (we'll have more to say about this in Chapter 7), you're really signing up with all the local agents. And chances are that one of

them may already be working with a buyer who is looking for a home just like yours.

3. **Agents provide professional advice and service.** Finally, in today's world, there's a lot of paperwork and tricky decisions required to sell a home. Presumably, an agent can guide you successfully through this minefield. Most sellers prefer to use an agent simply because of the peace of mind it brings.

## How Do You Find an Agent?

You won't have trouble finding an agent—there are close to a million of them. However, you may have trouble finding an agent who will do just the right job for you.

The right agent will be able to work with you to get the house sold and will work hard on your particular home. (Remember that good agents have many listings and can't devote all of their time to just one and still make a living.)

If you're looking for a good agent, here are some suggestions:

- **Get a recommendation.** Perhaps you have a friend, relative, neighbor, or associate who recently bought or sold a home and was very satisfied with the agent. Get the name and talk to that agent. You may have a winner.
- **Check with a local real estate office.** You want someone who knows the local real estate, especially your neighborhood. This person most likely will already be familiar with your model home, will know recent prices, and may be working with buyers looking to purchase nearby.
- **Look on the Internet.** Local offices which have a big presence on the Internet may be particularly active. Just remember, the most important thing is the specific agent you hire, not the office. It's your agent who will work hard to sell your property . . . or not.

Once you find an agent who can communicate well with you and who knows the market, you can consult with him or her on what homes are selling for in your area, as well as what additional prep work you may need to do. Having a good agent is like having a good and knowledgeable friend who's on your side when it comes time to sell your home. (Check Chapter 6 for questions to ask your agent before you hire him or her.)

## Step 4: Promote It

To some extent, all selling is a numbers game. Expose your property to enough people and sooner or later one of them will think it's just right and buy it. That's one of the big reasons that you list your home with an agent. Presumably that agent can expose your property to lots of buyers.

However, not all agents are equally skilled at promoting property. And some sellers choose to promote the property themselves when it's sold FSBO (For Sale By Owner) or through a discount broker who only does a limited amount of the selling work.

As a consequence, it always comes back to you, the seller, to be sure that your property is adequately promoted. Here are the basic five promotional tools you should use (or see that your agent uses):

1. **Put it on the MLS.** The Multiple Listing Service is a cooperative that allows all realtors to work on your house. (They split the commission, as we'll see in Chapter 6.) Thus, when you put your home on the MLS you not only have the agent with whom you signed working on your home, you have all the Realtors in the area working on it. Most agents will automatically put your home on the MLS when you list, but not necessarily. Make sure you ask to see that multiple listing is part of the listing. You can also put it on the MLS using a "Flat Fee MLS Listing" through

some agents who will not provide any service to you—just the listing. (It's a kind of FSBO plan.) The flat fee is typically under $400, the total amount you would pay the listing agent. (To make a sale, you would, of course, need to pay the selling agent a commission. See Chapter 7 for more details.)

2. **Put out a sign.** Be sure that you (or your agent) put a good looking "For Sale" sign on your property. Historically, this is one of the most effective sales tools, although some cities restrict the size and number of such signs. You may want to include a few relevant details on the sign as a further enticement, such as "View" or "Pool" or "Large Lot."

3. **Send out flyers.** These should include a picture of your home as well as such vital statistics as square footage, bedrooms, bathrooms, amenities, and so forth. Put a box on your yard sign to hold the flyers so potential buyers can stop by and take one. Send them to all your neighbors. (One of them may be looking to move, buy a nearby home for a relative, or pick up an investment property). Post the flyers in stores, libraries, and whatever bulletin boards allow them.

4. **Advertise online.** When you list on the MLS, normally your home is picked up and shown on www.realtor.com, the most widely viewed real estate Web site by buyers. Also, some properties are repeated on other sites such as AOL and Yahoo! You can list your property for free on craigslist.com. And there are many FSBO Web sites such as www.owners.com and www.fsbo.com that will list your property either for free or for a nominal fee. Don't overlook the Internet—most buyers check there first.

5. **Local newspaper advertising.** It may be old-fashioned, but it's still highly effective. Buyers check the newspaper for homes for sale. Is yours listed there? If you broker isn't

advertising, you should find out why. Perhaps you can arrange to pay for some advertising in exchange for a lower commission. Or you will want to put up a few ads on your own if you're selling by owner.

## Step 5: Incentivize It

In a challenging market you have to give buyers a reason to act. They need a reason to make the move to buy, and then you need to be sure it's your house they're buying. There are many ways to do this, but here are a few that you definitely will want to consider. (These ideas are also discussed in greater detail in Chapter 10.)

**TRAP**

Many sellers worry about the cost of incentives. Don't. If they help sell your property, consider them simply a cost of sale. Remember to keep your eye on the donut (the sale) and not the hole (the cost of incentives).

- **Pay the buyer's points.** A "point" is 1 percent of the mortgage amount. Buyers typically pay anywhere from one to five points when they get a mortgage. If you pay the points for them, it cuts down on their cash requirements. It makes it easier for them to get into your house. Just think of it as a lowering of your price in order to get a sale.
- **Pay the buyer's other nonrecurring closing costs.** In addition to points, you can also pay the buyer's title insurance, escrow charges, and other fees. It usually amounts to a few thousand less for the buyer to come up with, which makes your home all the more financially attractive.
- **Pay down the buyer's interest rate.** Many lenders will allow this. By paying a one time, up-front fee to the buyer's lender, you can get the interest rate reduced for a number

of years. The more you pay, the lower the interest rate is reduced, and for more years. Offer it to buyers and watch them light up—you've just told them you'll cut their monthly payments! (Of course, you'll need to work with the buyer to come up with a lender who'll do this—just check with a good mortgage broker. See Chapter 9 for details.)

- **Throw in appliances, TV, or other goodies.** These incentives work best when the market is just slow, but there are still buyers around. They help buyers choose your home over a comparable one that your neighbor is trying to sell without incentives.

- **Finance it.** Finally, you can carry back the paper, most typically in the form of a second mortgage. This is particularly appealing to buyers who are challenged either in terms of credit or income. If they can't qualify for an institutional mortgage, you may give them a chance to buy by offering to carry the mortgage yourself. But be careful. The same reasons that make them a poor institutional mortgage risk may make them a poor risk for seller financing. (See Chapter 9 for more information.)

## Step 6: Price It to Market

We started with price in Step 1 and now we return to price in Step 6. The reason is simple: price is the single most important element in any sale.

**TIP**

In any market, pricing is crucial to finding a buyer.

We already saw how to get a price using comparables and a CMA. However, a CMA only tells you what the market was a few months ago. It doesn't tell you what the market is right now. Or where it will be a few months from now.

Decades ago, the real estate housing market was relatively stable. If you got a CMA, it was good for at least six months, simply because homes didn't go up or down in value very rapidly.

That's not been the case in recent years. During the housing bubble between roughly 2000 and 2006, prices roared up as much as 25 percent a year. And during the more recent housing collapse, they've plummeted—although not as rapidly—but still by sometimes double digit amounts. (That's why during the bubble there were multiple offers—the houses were priced too low for the market; and more recently why there are often lowball offers—the houses are priced too high for the market.)

Prices are in flux. It's unlikely you'll be able to get today the amount you could have gotten for your home even just three or two or even one month ago. Prices may have fallen (or risen) since then.

Thus, in order to price your home to sell, you'll have to price it to market. That means projecting where the market will be when your home is listed or otherwise goes on sale.

**TIP**

If your home doesn't sell right away, you'll have to adjust your price to keep up with the market. Savvy sellers adjust their price every two weeks to a month.

## How Do You Project Prices?

While no one knows with any degree of certainty where prices will be tomorrow, it is possible to look at trends. We can identify trends and at least say, "If prices keep going the way they've been, here's where they will likely be in a few weeks and a few months."

Some of ways to identify trends in the housing market is to look at its trend setters.

## Identifying Market Trends

- **Watch the inventory of unsold homes.** The National Association of Realtors and local real estate boards track how many listed homes are unsold at any given time. Usually, when the inventory is rising, prices will soon be falling. (This only stands to reason, as increased inventory means a greater supply, which tends to drive values down.) When the inventory falls, on the other hand, price increases are usually not far behind.

Inventory statistics are widely available online, in newspapers, and from agents. They are typically given in several forms:

- **Average days on market.** This tells you how long it typically takes for a house to sell.
- **Months of inventory.** This tells you how many months it would take to sell out the current inventory of homes, provided no more homes came onto the market.
- **Rising/Falling inventory.** This tells you whether the inventory of unsold homes is increasing or decreasing.

**TRAP**

Sometimes in a falling market, the inventory of unsold homes will seem to stabilize for a time. Beware of a false bottom. The reason the number of unsold houses may not be increasing is that sellers who couldn't sell have taken their homes off the market—and other sellers, fearing the bad market, aren't putting theirs on. Any uptick in price, however, could launch a wave of new properties offered "for sale," thus dramatically increasing inventory.

- **Read the newspapers.** Papers love to report on falling (or rising) real estate markets. Often it's on the front page, but you should find it in the business or real estate sections at least.

  Depending on the how well the paper reports, the facts and figures could be quite informative, with opinions from experts on how long the housing market will continue to decline or rise, and by how many percentage points. While you can't entirely rely on these figures, they can be helpful.

- **Check online sites.** Some Internet sites can be particularly helpful in explaining trends. Try www.foreclosure.com or www.realtytrac.com for information on foreclosures. As foreclosures increase, they put downward pressure on the market. Try www.bankrate.com for general financial news. If the country is moving toward recession, there will be job losses, which translate into downward pressure on housing (fewer buyers). If it's moving toward expansion, we're likely to see increased sales (more buyers). Try www.hsh.com for information on mortgages. As mortgage interest rates decline, it becomes easier for borrowers to buy and there are more sales. As mortgage interest rates go up, the opposite occurs.

- **Talk to agents.** Active agents are keenly aware of market conditions and can convey to you in just a few words whether the market is hot, cold, or moving sideways.

**TRAP**

Be aware that agents tend to be almost universally optimistic. If they paint a rosy picture that doesn't seem to jibe with your other sources, take it with a grain of salt.

## Get Ahead of the Curve

You've done your homework and you're now projecting that the market is heading down, up or sideways. What do you do with that information?

You take the CMA price you arrived at in step one and adjust down or up. (Make no adjustment in a sideways market.) For example, you've determined that prices are falling at an annual rate of about 6 percent a year in your neighborhood and everything you've read suggests they'll continue to fall for at least the next 12 months.

Your CMA is based on sales of homes going back six months. How do you adjust it?

You simply reduce the price for your house from your CMA by a half year's decline, or 3 percent. That's what it's likely worth now, not six months ago when the comps sold.

Then you go a step further. You project what your house will be worth three months from now, a figure of approximately 1.5 percent (for three more months of decline) and you deduct that from your price as well.

Let's take an example. Your CMA says your home is worth $200,000. Now you reduce that by 3 percent, or $6,000, to bring you to the current price. And you reduce it by another 1.5 percent to project it out three months into the future, or $3,000. Your asking price should be $191,000.

It's definitely not a pleasant thing to do. But, then again, it's better than letting your home sit unsold on the market because you've priced it too high.

**TRAP**

No, it's not that exact. But, it's a great rule of thumb to follow.

You want to get ahead of the curve when you're selling in any market because that will entice buyers to make good offers. When prices are declining, if you're ahead of the curve and asking lower than even today's market price, buyers will see you as reasonable and as offering good value. You'll likely get a sale. (If you project that prices will increase instead of decline, then ask more and you'll be able to pocket more profit.)

**TIP**

Buyers in a declining market are afraid to pay even market price, because they worry that whatever they pay today, their house will be worth less tomorrow. Thus, to sell you need to give them tomorrow's price.

### Reprice Regularly

If for whatever reason, your home doesn't sell right away, don't stick with the price you originally put on it. Reprice it at least every month and perhaps as often as every two weeks.

Remember, prices rarely stay constant these days. They tend to always be in a state of flux. And you have to follow them, if you want to sell.

## The Bottom Line

If you want to sell your home in any market, here once again are the six steps:

1. Compare it                    _____
2. Prep it                       _____
3. Agentize it                   _____
4. Promote it                    _____
5. Incentivize it                _____
6. Price it to market            _____

# Tough Love on Pricing

There are some things people just won't tell you. Your agent won't tell you, because she doesn't want to lose a listing.

Your best friend won't tell you, because he's worried you'll get mad at him. (And is a home sale worth a friendship?)

Your spouse won't tell you, because he or she probably doesn't know, either.

Even your neighbors won't tell you, because they're hoping you'll sell for a fortune, which will make their homes worth more.

What's the big secret?

At the risk of making you unhappy, dear reader, I'll spill the beans. The secret is that you're asking too much for your house!

## What You Won't Find in This Chapter

In this book's other chapters, you'll find commiseration, understanding, and even affection for the person who wants to sell. But in this chapter, you're going to find only one thing: the hard, sometimes unwelcome facts that will make it possible for you to get that house of yours sold.

Remember in the last chapter, how I said that the single most important factor in getting a sale in this challenging market was price? Here we're going to get down to bare knuckles on how to get to that price.

## The Equity That Was

Let's begin with the price you arrived at after going through steps one and six of the last chapter. Let's say it was $250,000.

However, at the peak of the market, you know your home was worth $400,000. (You know because that's what the highest-priced home in your neighborhood sold for a few years back.) So in your heart of hearts, you know that's what your home is truly worth.

But, what about that $250,000 figure arrived at after doing a CMA (Comparative Market Analysis) and pricing it to market (getting ahead of the curve) we learned in Chapter 1?

I'm sure you're thinking to yourself that this Irwin guy has a few good ideas, but just because he says it doesn't make it so. Why give away all that equity? The house just has to be worth more.

**TRAP**

Equity is only measured in snapshots. It changes year to year, month to month, and in some cases, even day to day. When someone says their equity is *x* number of dollars, be sure to ask them, "On what date?"

I'm certainly the last person on earth who would suggest you give away any equity. However, I'm also the guy who's telling you to step back and take a look at what your equity really is—and is not.

## What Your Equity Is Not

- It's not the highest or lowest price your home was ever evaluated at in the past.
- It's not what it was at the peak (or the bottom) of the market, unless that happens to be right now.
- It's not what it was two years ago, one year ago, six months ago, or even last week.

The good way to think of equity is like the value of a stock. When the market (and your stock) is up, your interest or equity in it also goes up. When it's down, your equity in it declines as well.

The market fluctuates and so does your stock's value. Of course, when its value is high, it makes you feel good. And when it's low, it tends to make you feel bad. But that's the roller coaster that's the stock market.

But—and here's the important part—you never really lock in your equity in the stock until you sell it. It's only on that day that you know how much you truly made or lost on your investment.

A house is the same. As the market goes up or down, so too does the value of your home . . . and your equity in it. One year your equity may be $150,000. The next it could be $100,000 . . . or $200,000.

However, all figures are potential until you sell. It's only when you sell that you lock in your equity.

That's why it makes little sense to try to get out the equity you had in your house a year ago. That past equity no longer exists. Of course, you may reasonably say you lost equity by failing to sell when the market was higher. (And we'll all join you in a moment of silence for lost opportunities.) But, it's simply wishful thinking to believe that you can get today the equity you had yesterday. That equity is gone.

## Your Equity Will Come Back!

Some sellers, pining for their lost equity, hope to redeem it by waiting. They feel if they wait long enough, their lost equity will return.

I've got no argument with that. If there's one thing the real estate market in America has proven, it's that in the long run, it always goes higher.

But how long does it take? It could be a year. Two years. Five years. Or?

If you've got the time and want to put your life on hold, stay put. Take your home off the market. Wait. Eventually the market will surely catch up to where it was—and you are. And you'll be able to sell for the equity you believe you have in your home.

Alternatively, if you can handle the often negative cash flow that may be involved, rent out your home, and move into what is often a compromise property. (Compromised because you'll have payments on two homes and won't be taking out whatever equity you do have left in your old house. It won't be available to plunk down on your next house.)

Or, bite the bullet. Admit your equity is what it is (even if you're upside down and it's negative—see Chapter 5) and get rid of that house. Sell it for what it's worth today. Move on with your life.

## What About . . . ?

You may feel that I'm being a bit harsh, after all the sweat and money you put into your home. If so, here's a simple list to go through. It tells you what does *not* determine the price of your house—and what does.

### What Does *Not* Determine a Home's Price

- How much you paid for it
- How big your mortgage(s) is
- How high your taxes are
- How hard you've worked on it
- How much you love it
- What you think it's worth
- What the assessor thinks it's worth
- What an agent or an appraiser thinks it's worth

### What *Does* Determine a Home's Price

- What the market says it's worth—what a buyer is willing to pay for it.

**TIP**

It's not necessarily what a buyer *wants* to pay that determines price. It's what a buyer is *willing* to pay after all the negotiations and counteroffers.

## Useful Pricing Terms

I hope I've convinced you of the true meaning of equity and price. Remember, being realistic when it comes to value is the most important thing in selling your home in any market.

Along the way to pricing your home correctly, you're likely to run into a number of terms which could be useful. It's important that you have an understanding of them so that they don't throw you.

**Average Sales Price.** If you add up the prices for all the homes sold and divide that by the number of properties, that's the average sales price. It is sometimes quoted in the press, but what's usually given is the national or state average. Since all real estate is local, it may not even be close to the average price in your neighborhood, which is what's important to you.

**Median Sales Price.** This is the price above which half the homes have recently sold for, and below which the other half of the homes recently sold for. It's a much more frequently quoted figure in the press. Again, look for the most local numbers. Since the demand for homes is shaped like a pyramid (bigger on the bottom than on the top) and if your home is priced below the median sales price (or at least close to it), you've got a bigger pool of buyers to work with than if you're far above the median.

**Average List Price.** Add up the asking prices for all the homes recently sold and divide that by the number of homes, and you'll get the average listed price. By itself, this is not very useful. But, the difference between it and the average sales price (noted above), tells you how much sellers are knocking off their asking price in order to get a sale.

For example, if the average list price in your area for homes sold was $300,000, yet the average sales price was $275,000, it tells you that on average, sellers are getting around 8 or 9 percent less than they are asking. This usually only occurs in a falling market. In a rising market, sellers typically get much closer to their asking price— and sometimes above! It gives you something to aim for.

**TRAP**

You normally won't be able to learn the actual sales price on a home (or at least what amount buyers and sellers agreed upon) until the house actually closes escrow. Agents and sellers don't usually release that information prematurely, in case the current deal falls through and they have to start negotiations over with a new buyer.

## The Bottom Line

Selling a home is actually quite simple. Do all the stuff we talked about in the last chapter. And then price it right. If you do that, it will sell in any market.

# Finding an Agent Who Will Work Hard for You

A good, hard working agent will do all of the following:

- Help you with pricing
- Promote your property to other agents
- Find buyers and make a deal
- Competently handle all the paperwork
- Protect you throughout the transaction (and afterward)
- Get a sale
- And not cost an arm and a leg!

If you consider these requirements, you'll quickly come to the conclusion that the quality of the agent you choose is pretty important. A good agent will more than earn back the money you'll pay. A poor agent, while perhaps saving you money, can get you into more trouble than you'd ever imagine.

# Where Can You Find a Good Agent?

A good first step is to solicit recommendations. Ask your friends if they know people who have recently sold their home. There are so many agents around (close to 1 percent of the population in some areas) that almost everybody knows one. Did the sellers have a good experience? Would they use the agent again? Do they have any reservations about the agent?

If you can't get a recommendation, then it's up to you to find an agent on your own. Finding any old agent is easy. Just put a FSBO (For Sale By Owner) sign on your front lawn. You'll have agents climbing all over you trying to get your listing. Finding a *good* agent, however, is a bit more challenging.

I don't recommend starting out with a sign on your front lawn. Rather, check out a real estate office that's nearby. Being close is important because, presumably, the agents will know the immediate area well. Walk in and tell the receptionist or the salesperson who greets you that you want to talk to the broker. (Don't explain why, yet.)

## Visit a Nearby Real Estate Office

When the broker appears, explain that you are thinking of listing your house. You want to list with an office that's *active*. In fact, you'd like to list with the best salesperson (not lister) in the office.

But for now, you want to learn something about the office itself. For example, how many listings does the office currently have? If the office is active, the broker will be delighted to point out the many listings. If the office is a dud, there won't be many— or any. Leave if that's the case.

**TRAP**

Be sure to ask for listings taken by agents in *this* office. Don't be fooled if the broker simply takes out a book and shows you all the listings on the MLS. None of them may belong to that office.

Now ask how many of its *own* listings this office has sold in the past six months. The broker should know exactly. If the agents haven't sold any, or there's any hemming and hawing, leave.

Along the way, listen carefully to what the broker says. Is there one name, one agent, who keeps popping up? Is that agent, in fact, the best seller in the office?

At the end of your brief discussion, ask the broker who would be the best seller in the office in terms of sales (not listings). Most brokers will chuckle at your audacity, but will also probably give you a straight answer. (Is it the same name that kept popping up in your earlier conversation?)

## Get Personal

Now go see that person. Introduce yourself and ask not only how many properties he or she has sold, but how many were listed in the past six months. (You want to deal with a good salesperson, but also one who handles listings, not just the sales end of the business.)

Ask if you can have the phone numbers of the sellers of listings that this agent recently sold. Explain that you'd like to call them to see what they thought of the service.

This is the acid test. Most sellers never ask to see such a list. They wouldn't think of it. After all, it sounds like you're asking to see something confidential.

It's not confidential. Sales of homes are recorded and are public knowledge. If you want to take the time to go down to the hall of records, you can compile your own list of recent sellers.

A strong agent, one who will work for you, will be *delighted* to give you a list of recent sellers. After all, what does the agent do but please clients? A weak agent will give you reasons that she or he can't give out the list. Walk away.

TIP

In some offices, particularly the larger ones, the names of top agents, and in some cases even their pictures, often are posted on the walls. Just look carefully as you enter, and your search may be answered.

## Interview Prospective Agents

While knowing that the agent is a great salesperson is an enormous plus for you, you also need to know something more. You want to be sure the person is competent in the real estate business, honest in dealings, and reliable.

You may want to ask the following questions to help you determine these things:

### Agent Interview Questions

1. **"How long have you been in the real estate business?"**
   The learning curve for real estate is fairly long. The reason is that the number of transactions a person can become involved with at any one time is limited. Usually it takes three to five years for an agent to have acquired a well-rounded education. Five to ten years is better.

2. **"What professional organizations do you belong to?"**
   The minimum here should be the local real estate board and Multiple Listing Service, as well as the state and National Association of Realtors (NAR). The agent may also be a member of the chamber of commerce and local citizens' groups—both pluses.

3. **"What will you do to expedite the sale of my home?"**
   The answer here should be immediate, direct, and comprehensive. The agent should explain a plan of action that

he or she hopes will sell your house. The plan should include:

a.  Listing for a specified time. (Beware of agents who want to list for more than three months—you can always extend the listing later. But if they do a poor job, you're locked in for the term.)

b.  Promotion, including talking up the listing at the local real estate board.

c.  Advertising.

d.  Open houses.

Here's a checklist of the questions you can ask your future agent.

### Agent Interview Checklist

1.  How many houses listed in the last six months?    _____
2.  How many houses sold in the last six months?    _____
3.  Will make references available?    _____
4.  Fully licensed?    _____
5.  Works full-time in real estate?    _____
6.  Been in the business at least three to five years?    _____
7.  Is a Realtor and belongs to other organizations?    _____
8.  Offers a plan for selling my home?    _____
9.  Does not ask for an overly long listing?    _____
10. Knows my neighborhood?    _____
11. Will provide written/oral reports?    _____
12. Will market my property online?    _____
13. Will provide a CMA at no cost or obligation?    _____

## Should You Go with a Chain or an Independent Office?

Twenty or thirty years ago, virtually all real estate agents were independent. Today, the vast majority belong to a national chain such as

Century 21, RE/MAX, Coldwell Banker, Prudential, or some other national company. These are big names and big companies.

Thus, one of the first questions that most sellers ask is: should I go with a chain or with an independent?

The answer is that the question is often irrelevant. One of the best tips this book can give you is that you should go with the best agent you can find. If that agent happens to be associated with a chain, great. If the agent is independent, just as great.

Don't base your listing decision solely on the sign in front of the office.

### Advantages of a Franchise

- Chains usually offer at least minimal standards of performance. And if something should go wrong in your dealings with your individual agents, you can complain to someone higher up.
- One office tends to look like another, and in general, the agents tend to be fairly well trained.
- They have power in advertising and name brand recognition, which helps find buyers.
- Chains often offer long-distance moving assistance. List your home with a chain in one city and an agent from a linked chain in another city can already be looking for a new home for you.

### Advantages of the Independent Broker

- They can be more flexible when dealing with you. Often they can make their own decisions about cutting the commission, whereas an agent working for a chain may need special approval.
- Because they are independent, they often try to work harder.

## Hire the Agent, Not the Office

The agent who will make the most difference in getting your home sold is the one with whom you work directly. That's the agent who will take your listing, advise you on pricing, "talk up" your property to other agents (a very important function), conduct open houses, negotiate the deal, do the paperwork, and steer the transaction to a successful close.

You want someone who is reliable, trustworthy, competent, and hard working. Find that person and you've got a good agent. Chances are they'll be working for a good office.

## Negotiating the Commission

Everything in real estate is negotiable, including the commission.

Once you've decided to list your home for sale and have found the right agent, it's time to negotiate the commission and the listing terms.

If this surprises you, you're not alone. Most first-time buyers and even a great many experienced ones aren't aware that commissions and listings are fully negotiable. They just assume there's a "going rate" and the agent will give them that.

Nothing could be further from the truth. There is no going rate, and every agent will negotiate for the listing terms, conditions, and commission rate. Not every agent will necessarily accept what you may want to offer, but all agents should listen and consider it.

**TIP**

If you find an agent who doesn't want to negotiate, listen carefully. Maybe, just maybe, the agent is so good that he or she can command a higher price. But before you list with such an agent, you'd better have some pretty solid indications that they can deliver a buyer at your price and terms in short order.

It is both illegal and unethical in all areas of the country for a real estate board to "set" a standard rate of commission.

## Can You Get a Lower Commission?

Most rates of commission today for *listing* single-family residential property range from a low flat rate of about $400 to a high of 3 percent of the selling price. That's the amount that goes to the listing office. Of course, there's also the amount that goes to the office that brings in a buyer. This is typically anywhere from 2 to 3 percent. Thus the total commission you're likely to pay runs the gamut from about $400 to a total of 6 percent of the selling price. (We'll have more to say about the difference between listing and selling offices shortly.)

### Typical Commission Range

| To Listing Office | To Selling Office |
| --- | --- |
| $400 to 3 percent | 2 to 3 percent |

Many sellers erroneously assume that all agents automatically charge 6 percent. Today the *average* commission nationwide is closer to 5 percent.

## Flat Fee MLS

At the lowest end of the scale are special discount brokers who will list your property and put it on the MLS for a flat fee, typically under $400. (Of course, in order to induce other agents to work on the listing, you'll want to offer a reasonable fee to those who bring in the buyer—typically 2 to 3 percent.)

The flat fee MLS lister will typically do nothing else for you. Rather, you'll be responsible for all the work of the selling agent. This is equivalent to selling on your own. (See Chapter 7 on selling by owner for where to find these flat rate brokers.)

## Discount Brokers

In many areas of the country, discount brokers are available, many claiming to offer full service. These brokers often charge anywhere from a flat fee of several thousand dollars to as much as 2.5 percent of the sales price.

Why not go with a discounter, if it can save you money?

Just be sure you understand what you're getting. A discounter may or may not provide full service. For a severe discount (as in the case of the flat fee MLS), no services are usually provided. For a higher fee, some or all services may be.

Keep in mind, we're talking here strictly about the services performed by the lister for you. These are separate from the services performed by the broker who finds the buyer. You normally pay for these as well.

But, you may ask, why pay for the buyer's broker? Why not just pay for the lister?

### A True Experience

I was looking to buy a rental home. I was working with an agent who was showing me this house and that. When we got back to the office, we went through the listings on his computer and I noticed he always seemed to skip over some. Since they were in my price range, I asked him to stop at one of them.

When he complied, I saw one that seemed perfect. When I asked him why we hadn't looked at this home, he said he didn't think it was right for me. Then I looked at the listing . . . and the listing commission rate. It was $500. The seller wasn't willing to pay the agent who brought in the buyer almost anything.

The truth is, the home wasn't right for *him!*

TIP

In theory, the agent should never shy away from a house which might be ideal for the buyers, but which provides a lower commission. That's unethical and may even be illegal. Actual practice, however, is sometimes considerably different from theory.

You want to expedite the sale of your home, and that means getting as many agents to work on it as possible. That's why you want to offer a reasonable commission to the office that finds the buyer. You don't want to be that property that always seems to get skipped over.

## Can You Handle the Reduced Service?

As noted, many discount brokers reduce the services they offer to you in exchange for a reduced listing commission. They may not be willing to negotiate with the buyers. That could be up to you. Or they could ask you to pay for advertising your property. Or they may not be willing to work with buyers to secure financing or to move a deal through escrow.

In short, a discounter may not offer all the services you assume are available. Are you okay with that? After all, perhaps you don't need full service. Perhaps what you need is partial service, because you're selling your home on your own.

My advice is to let yourself be guided by your needs and by what the discounter offers. If you want a broker to completely handle your sale, go to a full-service, full-commission broker. On the other hand, if you're willing to handle some of the heavy lifting yourself, then by all means try a discounter.

**TRAP**

Be sure you know what you're getting. Find out exactly which services a discounter offers, and get it in writing.

### When You Should Use a Discounter

- You want to pay a lower commission.
- You don't want or need a full-service broker.
- You're willing to do some of the work yourself.

### When You Should Use a Full-Service Agent

- You want maximum exposure and advertising.
- You don't want to do any of the sales work yourself.
- You're willing to pay the price.

## What About Asking a Full-Service Agent to Take Less?

There's no reason that you can't tell an agent what the maximum commission is that you'll pay. For example, you can say, "I'm willing to pay a 2 percent listing commission and a 2 percent selling commission for a total of 4 percent—not a penny more! Are you willing to work for that amount?"

Now listen carefully to how the agent replies. Some will say that they can't afford to do a good, full-service job for that price and may decline. Or they may recommend a discount broker. That's an agent who knows what he or she is worth.

Others may say that, yes, they'll consider working for what you offer. But they don't like it. And they may only take your listing grudgingly.

I would be suspicious of these agents. They may also know what they're worth—and it could be a lot less than other agents in terms of ability to deliver a ready, willing, and able buyer.

## Why Are Real Estate Commissions So High?

Even though the agent may make a good case for a 6 or even 7 percent commission, one can't help but wonder why commissions in general are so high. Few people remember that back in the 1950s, the average *maximum* commissions were generally around 5 percent. By the 1990s they had climbed to the 6 and sometimes 7 percent range.

Back in the 1950s, the average house also cost only around $15,000. That means that at 5 percent, the total commission was only $750 (for both lister and seller).

Today it's around $200,000. At 6 percent, that translates to $12,000.

Today's commission is over 16 times higher. Why?

Part of the answer is simple inflation. Things cost many times more today than they did 60 years ago.

Another part of the answer is better agents. Back in 1950, all an agent had to do to sell real estate was pass a short test, rent an office, and put out a sign. Today, agents' tests often last several days. There may be college or night school requirements, as well as apprentice-ship requirements. Even the cost of the license itself has gone up.

Finally, there are additional selling costs today. Today's agents must pay for errors and omission insurance and sometimes several kinds of malpractice insurance. Also, they must have an attorney on call, something that almost no one had back in 1950.

Thus, when you are asked to pay a higher commission today, you'll know that it's not all going just into the agent's pocket.

## Commission Splitting

Most people know that agents split commissions. But many peo-ple do not know how that split works or the discount agents are able to give them.

It's important to remember that while you may deal with only one listing agent, by the time your house is sold, there may be as many as four agents involved. (In the vast majority of cases at least two agents are involved.)

Typically, the single commission you pay is split among all the agents involved. The splits vary, with 50-50 being typical.

Let's say you sell your home for $200,000. There happen to be two different brokers involved and two different salespeople. (You listed with a salesperson and the buyer bought through a salesperson.)

Here's how a typical split of a 6 percent commission might work out:

**Typical Commission Split**

| To Listing Agents | To Selling Agents |
| --- | --- |
| 1.5% ($3,000) to salesperson | 1.5% ($3,000) to salesperson |
| 1.5% ($3,000) to broker | 1.5% ($3,000) to broker |

Instead of a whopping 6 percent or $12,000 paid to one person, four agents each split it up, getting $3,000 apiece. It's important to keep that in mind the next time you're tempted to tell your agent to cut the commission in half, or in this case by $6,000. That may actually be twice as much as the total he or she gets!

**TIP**

Sometimes really good agents will negotiate a better split with their broker. Splits of as high as 80 or 90 percent of the broker's commission (half of the total) are not uncommon for top agents.

## Understanding the Listing Agreement

In addition to agreeing on a commission rate, there's the matter of agreeing to the terms of the listing. These are spelled out in a listing agreement that the agent will want you to sign.

There are a variety of listing types which an agent can offer you. (No, there isn't just one standard listing that they all use.)

Each type of listing has its own pluses and minuses and should be considered in light of your specific needs. The listing agreement will normally say right on its face which type it is. You can negotiate the type of listing agreement with the agent.

## Exclusive Right-to-Sell

An exclusive right-to-sell listing is the type that almost all agents prefer. It is also the type that many listing services prefer. It means the following: *If the agent or anyone else (including you) sells the house, you owe the agent a commission.* This includes people to whom you showed the house while the listing was in effect, even though you didn't sell the house until a limited time after the listing expired.

In other words, with this type of listing you ensure the agent a commission if the house is sold. The only way the agent cannot get a commission during the listing is if there is no sale. Sellers tend to dislike this type of commission because they feel it's unfair. Agents, on the other hand, like it because they feel protected. Most are willing to put forth 100 percent effort only if they get this type of listing.

## Exclusive Agency

*If the agent sells the house, you owe a commission. If you sell it to someone the agent (or a subagent) didn't show it to, you don't owe anything.*

Now, you may be thinking, that's a listing more to my liking.

Yes and no. Agents have good reasons for not liking this type of listing. They may bring buyers to your home who tell them they're not interested in purchasing. Later, the buyers come to you and negotiate a sale. You claim no commission is due because you had no knowledge that the agent showed these buyers the home. They dealt directly with you. The agent claims that a commission is due because he or she found the buyers.

In this case, the agent is right. But to get that commission, the agent might have to go to arbitration or even to court. Along the way, there's certain to be hard feelings, and agents are very concerned about their reputation in a community. They don't like it to be known that they had to put pressure on a seller to collect even a justified commission. Thus, most agents simply won't work (or won't work hard) on this type of listing.

An exclusive agency listing is sometimes appropriately used when you think you might come up with a buyer or buyers who might be interested in purchasing, but who haven't yet committed. You want to list the property and get it onto the market, but you want to exclude paying a commission for those buyers you might personally find.

## Open Listing

*You agree to pay a commission to any broker who brings you a buyer or to pay no commission if you find the buyer.*

Some sellers think this is a good type of listing, because you can give it to any agent.

Most agents, however, won't devote 10 minutes of time to this kind of listing. If buyers should show up whom they can't interest in any other piece of property, then they'll bring them to you in a last chance effort at a commission. The opportunity to do work and not get paid for it is so great here that agents in general just don't want to bother with this type of listing.

About the only time it's used is in bare land, when the chances of selling are very slim and it could take years to produce a buyer.

You might simply let every agent know that the property is for sale and you'll pay a commission, but you're not willing to give any one of them an "exclusive."

## Guaranteed-Sale Listing

A guaranteed-sale listing isn't a separate type of listing. Rather it's any of the above, but is usually the exclusive right to sell. *The listing simply includes a separate clause, which says that if the property isn't sold by the end of the listing term, then the agent agrees to buy it from you for a set price (usually the listing price or lower), less the commission.*

Although widely used at one time, this type of listing is often frowned upon today because of the potential conflict of interest. The reason is simple. While an honest agent can use the guaranteed-sale listing to induce you to list, a dishonest agent can use it to gain a larger-than-expected commission.

A dishonest agent may induce an unwary seller to list, then take no action to sell the property. When the listing expires, the agent buys the house at a previously guaranteed low price and later resells at a much higher price. This is particularly a problem when the listing calls for the agent to buy the property for less than the listed price (justified by the supposed "fact" that because it didn't sell for the listed price, that price must have been too high).

If your agent suggests this type of listing, insist on the following (which may already be legally required in your state):

1. The agent can buy the property only for the listed price. No less.
2. The agent has to inform you, and you have to agree in writing to the price, if the agent resells the property to someone else within one year of your sale to the agent.
3. The agent must buy the property. The agent can't sell it to a third party in escrow, unless you get all the proceeds, less the agreed-upon commission.

## Net Listing

The net listing is by far the most controversial type. *You agree up front on a fixed price for the property. Everything over that price goes to the agent.*

You agree to sell for $100,000. If the agent brings in a buyer for $105,000, the agent gets $5,000 as the commission. But if the agent brings in a buyer for $150,000 the agent gets $50,000 for a commission!

The opportunities to take advantage of a seller here should be obvious. An unscrupulous agent could get a listing for a low price and then sell for a high one, getting an unconscionable commission.

A net listing is sometimes useful for a "hopeless" property. For one reason or another, the property isn't salable. So the seller tells the agent, "Be creative. Find a buyer. Here's what I want. Everything else is yours." In such an arrangement, you as the seller should insist (if state law doesn't already require it) that you be informed of the final selling price and that you agree in writing to it.

The easiest way to handle a net listing is to simply avoid it.

## Which Type of Listing Should You Give?

The type of listing that's best for you depends, of course, on your situation and that of your property. It's a surprise to most sellers that in 95 percent of the cases, the listing that is likely to get you the best results is the exclusive right to sell.

**TIP** In the trade, allowing other agents to work on a listing is called "cobroking" it. Be sure your agent agrees to cobroke your property with all other agents. You want everyone to work on it, not just one agent.

In it, you do give up your right to sell the property by yourself. But in exchange, you get the best chance of having the agent put forth his or her best efforts in completing the sale.

If you give this type of listing, you want to be sure that your agent puts your house on a listing service, such as the Multiple Listing Service or whatever cooperative system is in use in your area. That guarantees that your house will get the widest possible exposure.

**TRAP**

An old line that some agents use is: "To give you a better chance at a quick sale, I'll hold back the listing from the cooperative listing service for a few weeks. This means that all the agents in my office will work harder on it. It's really a better opportunity for you, the seller." Don't believe it. It's just a ploy to give the listing agent a chance to sell your property exclusively without having to split the commission. During those few weeks before your house gets on the cooperative system, your agent may indeed be knocking himself out trying to sell it. But that's one agent. On the service, as many as 1,000 or more agents will be aware that your house is for sale. One of them may already have a buyer looking for just what you've got.

Don't let the agent "hold back" (also sometimes called "vest pocketing") your listing. Insist that it be given the widest, earliest possible exposure.

## Do You Understand the Listing Agreement?

The listing agreement is often several pages long and may contain a considerable amount of legalese. However, there are a number of points that it should contain and that you should watch out for.

### What to Look for in a Listing Agreement

1. **Price.** The listing agreement should specify the price you expect to receive for your property.
2. **Deposit.** The agreement should indicate how large a deposit you expect from a buyer. It should also indicate that the agent may hold the deposit, but that it is your money. Usually such agreements specify that if the buyer

doesn't go through with the deal, you and the agent split the deposit. However, you can insist that in that case the entire deposit is yours.

3. **Terms.** It's important that the terms you are willing to accept are spelled out. For example, if you want only cash, your listing agreement should say that. If you are willing to accept a second mortgage as part of the purchase price, it should specify that as well. In actual practice, this doesn't preclude an agent from bringing you a buyer who offers other terms. It just means you don't have to accept such a buyer.

4. **Title insurance.** Today almost all property sold has title insurance. The only questions are which title company to use and who is going to pay for it. The listing agreement usually specifies both. In most areas, title insurance costs are split between buyer and seller, although in some states the seller pays it. Find out what is commonly done in your area. Just be sure you don't pay for title insurance if you don't need to!

5. **Lockbox.** Buyers come by when they're ready, not when you're ready. Therefore, it's a good idea to allow the agent to show the property even when you're not home. Since there may be many cooperative agents, the common way of handling this is to have a lockbox installed. The listing agreement asks you to give permission for a lockbox.

   Be aware, however, that you are opening up your home to a great many people. Agents and buyers represent a broad spectrum of people. Just as in the general population, there are those who are scrupulously honest, as well as those who are dishonest in real estate. While the incidence of theft from homes with lockboxes installed is small, it does occasionally occur. Therefore, for the time you have a lockbox on your home you are well advised to remove all valuables. Note: In many listing agreements the agents specifically disclaim responsibility for loss due to having a lockbox improperly used.

6. **Sign.** You should give permission for the agent to install a reasonable sign in your front yard. It's an excellent method of attracting buyers, perhaps the best.

7. **Arbitration and attorney's fees.** Typically these agreements call for arbitration in case of a dispute and state that in the case of a lawsuit the prevailing party will have his or her attorney's costs paid by the losing party. Read this wording carefully. You may want to ask an attorney if you should sign or change it.

8. **Disclosure.** The listing agreement should also list the various disclosures that you as a seller must make to a buyer in your state. (These are discussed in Chapter 15.)

9. **Equal housing disclosure.** You must be in compliance with federal and state antidiscrimination laws when you list your property.

10. **Beginning and expiration date.** Perhaps the most critical part of the document is the clause that states when the listing you are giving expires. It should be a written-out date such as "June 1, 1997," not "in three months." If the date isn't inserted, the agent could insist that the listing you intended to be for three months is actually for much longer. I suggest never giving a listing for more than three months. In most markets, that should be enough time for a good agent to find a buyer. If there are extenuating circumstances, at the end of the three-month period, you might want to extend the listing for an additional three months. Or you might want to secure the services of a different agent.

11. **Commission.** The agreement will state the percentage of commission that you've agreed upon. Beware of a clause

right next to it, which may state something to the effect that if you take your house off the market for any reason, you owe the agent a fee that is then written in. This is a "liquidated damages" clause and it means that although you may not have to pay the full commission if you decide not to sell, you are committing yourself to paying something, often a substantial amount of money. Have your attorney check this out.

In addition to the listing agreement itself, most agents will provide you with an agent's disclosure document stating to whom the agent owes a fiduciary relationship—whether the agent is a seller's, buyer's, or dual agent. (See the following sections for an explanation.)

12. **Transaction fee.** This is a fee that brokers have been tacking on to be paid directly to their office. It's often around $500 over and above the commission.

Brokers charge this fee because they are paying their sales people higher commissions and leaving less for their overhead. However, that's their problem, not yours. I wouldn't sign any listing with a transaction fee in it.

## Listing Danger Signals

1. Agent wants listing for more than three months.
2. Agents insists on a commission higher than you want to pay.
3. Pressure on you to sign. (If brokers pressure you to sign the listing, think of what they'll do when a bad offer comes in.)
4. Lister willing to accept any sales price on the listing, even though you know it's too high. (The lister just wants you to sign and hopes that after a month or so when you can't sell, you'll drop your price.)

5. Hedging on the disclosures—saying that you don't really need to disclose a major defect. Failure to disclose a problem could result in the loss of the deal or even a lawsuit from a buyer.

6. Insisting on a listing (net or guaranteed sale) that allows them to make a higher commission without letting you know that they need your written permission.

7. Wanting your power of attorney to sign a deal. If you give up your power of attorney, the agent could accept an offer for you that you really don't want.

8. Charging a transaction fee. (Get this thrown out before you sign, or go to a different agency that doesn't charge it.)

**TIP**

It's important to be as specific as possible in the sales agreement about when the commission is earned. Typically, it's when the agent has produced a buyer who is "ready, willing, and able" to purchase. This, however, means that if you refuse to sell, you could still owe a commission. Sometimes sellers have negotiated a clause that says the commission is earned only when the sale is concluded and escrow closes.

**TRAP**

Beware of "listers." This is an agent who simply takes listings and lets them sit. Giving a longer listing might mean it will take longer to sell your house. My feeling is that no really good agent will normally want more than three months to sell a house in a stable market. After that, if the house doesn't sell, it could be overpriced or there could be some problem with it that will keep it from selling indefinitely—and it might not be worth the agent's time to bother with it. Wanting a long-term listing is a danger signal.

## The Agent's Responsibility

If you agree to list, what does the agent owe you in return?

Listing your home for sale is not a one-way street. You agree to pay a hefty commission to the agent. But that agent also agrees to give you something in return. That something should include:

### The Agent Owes You

Service

Loyalty

Diligence

Honesty

Disclosure of facts

Skill

Care

Some of the above may actually be stated in the listing agreement. Others are considered part of the agent's fiduciary responsibilities. All are considered examples of ethical conduct.

## Buyer's Agent versus Seller's Agent

As noted above, when you list with an agent, he or she owes you loyalty. That takes many forms. The clearest expression of loyalty is when the agent brings you a sales agreement for $195,000, but tells you that she or he has overheard the buyers say they would be willing to pay $200,000 for your house.

That little tidbit of information is worth $5,000 to you. Without it, you might have accepted the $195,000 offer. With it you hold out for $200,000—and get it.

Why should the agent be loyal to you and not to the buyer? Why should the agent tell you this information that was worth so much money?

### The Seller's Agent

The reason has to do with the agent's fiduciary (position of trust) relationship with you. It is incumbent upon the agent to tell you any fact that may help you in making your decision to sell.

It swings the other way too. If you tell the agent that you would be willing to accept $195,000 when you're asking $200,000—but not to tell any buyers that fact—the agent is obligated to follow your wishes. In fact, because of the fiduciary relationship, the agent is prohibited (in theory) from telling the buyers anything about price or terms that you do not specifically let the agent divulge.

In other words, a seller's agent is bound to you in ways that are definitely to your advantage.

**TRAP**

It's important not to get too smug about agency relationships. Not all agents stick to the letter of ethical conduct, and some agents (buyer's agents) may have fiduciary responsibilities to the buyers and not to you.

### The Buyer's Agent

Thus far, we've been talking about a seller's agent, the one who takes your listing. However, today many agents work for the buyer. They may even have the buyer sign an agreement like a listing.

As a seller, be wary of buyer's agents. They do not owe to you the same fiduciary responsibility as do seller's agents. Indeed, their responsibilities are reversed. They owe them to the buyers!

**TIP**

Whether an agent represents a buyer or a seller depends on who the agent declares for. Who pays the agent is not the issue. In fact, it's common for the seller's (your) agent to split the commission with the buyer's agent, so in effect, you're paying the buyer's agent!

## What Are Subagents?

When you list your property with an agent, he or she owes you a fiduciary responsibility as described above. But what if the agent puts your property on the MLS and suddenly 100 or 1000 agents are all working it? Do they owe you a fiduciary responsibility?

Yes—and no.

If they act as "subagents" (meaning that your agent delegates agency powers to them), then they owe you the same duties and responsibilities.

However, some agents act as buyer's agents, although they may still show your house and sell it off the listing service. These agents work for the buyer.

## What Are Dual Agents?

A dual agent is one who not only works for you, the seller, but also works for the buyer. The dual agent represents *both* parties. The crux of a dual agent's responsibilities can be found in telling on the price, just like the seller's agent could. Without permission, a dual agent may not tell a buyer that you're willing to take less *or tell you that the buyer is willing to pay more.*

In other words, the dual agent, because he or she owes both you and the buyer loyalty, may need to forgo disclosing some pricing information (and other similar crucial information) to either of you.

**TIP**

Agents must offer disclosure. An agent must tell you who he or she represents: you, the buyer, or both.

In the old days (several decades ago), the National Association of Realtors offered a code of ethics that was the forerunner of many of the rules of agency in most states. The code of ethics basically required that the agent deal fairly with all parties—buyers and sellers.

Today, however, virtually all states require that agents disclose to you whom they represent. Thus, when you sign your listing agreement, the agent may also present to you a second document which states, in effect, who he or she represents.

Usually you must not only read the disclosure, but sign to prove that you've read it.

## Which Type of Agent Do You Want?

Obviously, as a seller, you're not going to want a buyer's agent. But what about a seller's agent vs. a dual agent?

The answer should be straightforward. When you're selling your house, you want only a seller's agent. You want to be sure that the person with whom you list will represent you thoroughly.

That's all well and good. But what happens when your agent goes out and brings in a buyer, with no other agent involved? Does your agent now become a *dual* agent?

Maybe. It all comes out in disclosure. The agent who brings you the offer on your house should disclose what type of agent she or he is. If they don't disclose, you should demand a disclosure.

Whenever an offer is presented, demand to know who's represented by the agent presenting the offer. The agent should tell you. If the agent doesn't, presume that person is acting for the buyer and treat the offer as an adversarial one. Keep a tight lip and don't blab what you might take, if it's less than is being offered.

The point to understand here is that the agent determines whom she or he represents. Your goal is to find out who it is and then act accordingly.

# 14 Days to Shaping Up Your House for Sale

Fixing up, cleaning up, and staging can involve little things that make a big difference. Often we don't even realize the simple things we can do to make our house more salable.

But what should you do? And how will you find time to do it?

Here's a two-week home shape up plan that anyone can handle. You can do the work yourself in the evening or on weekends. Or you can hire it out. Either way, it will end up making your home more appealing to potential buyers.

## Day 1: Prepare the Front

Work first on the hedges and the lawn.

There are two purposes here. The first is to cut back on all that growth that's accumulated over the years so that buyers can more easily see your house. After all, they're presumably interested in purchasing a home, not a forest.

The second is to make sure that the lawn, which in most houses occupies more than half the front, looks neat. Of course, if there are brown spots or areas where the grass had died, you'll want to reseed (or sod), add fertilizer, and water, water, water.

The reason you'll want to start with the hedges and the lawn is that it takes them the longest to get into shape. After all, they have to grow to look nice.

## Day 2: Paint the Front

Unless you've had your home painted within the last year, it's going to need some work, especially in the front. Forget about "touching it up." After a year of exposure to the sun, the paint will have faded to the point where attempting to spot-paint any discoloration, flaking, peeling, and so on will only end up giving your home a blotchy look. Bite the bullet and paint the entire front. It will make the presentation of your home look terrific in terms of "curb appeal," that all-important first impression.

**TIP**

We've all heard the adage, "You never get a second chance to make a good first impression." The point is well taken. Attitudes toward people and homes are usually fixed and sometimes unchangeable with that first glance. With regard to homes, that first impression is called "curb appeal." It means how well your home shows itself off when that potential buyer drives up the very first time. That's why painting and polishing up the front of your home is so important.

If you're going to repaint with different colors, choose carefully. They should blend in well with the neighborhood décor and style. If your home is more than 10 years old, be especially careful about simply repainting using the old colors. Color trends change and what was modern and fresh looking a decade ago probably looks stale and old-fashioned today.

Check with a color expert, typically found at a good paint store. They should be able to give you some useful suggestions. (Try Benjamin Moore, www.benjaminmoore.com; Dun Edwards, www.dunedwards.com; or Sherwin-Williams, www.sherwin-williams.com, for starters.) Also, check with any local homeowners association about restrictions on paint colors. You may also want to check with your local building/planning department regarding paint color restrictions in your home's CC&Rs—conditions, covenants, and restrictions—that run with the land.

## Day 3: Paint the Trim

Assuming that you began trimming the hedges on a Friday, you can spend the weekend painting the front and trim of your home. Allow two days for the painting. Even with fast drying water-based paints, you'll want to do the walls the first day and the trim the second. Don't let the trim paint bleed into the wall paint.

Select a good complimentary color for the trim. Again, paint stores have excellent color charts that show you which trim colors go best with which basic colors. While you'll certainly want to select a neutral color that will appeal (or at least not offend) most buyers, you may also want to be just a little bit rakish, so that your house will stand out from its neighbors. See above for concerns with homeowners associations and CC&Rs.

## Day 4: Clean Outside

TIP

In a hot market, buyers tend to overlook a lot about a house's condition. In a cold market, however, everything becomes a deal point, which provides a reason to knock down the price or walk away. Don't give the buyer deal points by having a house that's in an unclean condition.

Start with cleaning the outside. Driveway cleaning can come down to putting on a new coating on an asphalt driveway or using cleaners to remove stains from a cement driveway. If the driveway is seriously cracked, however, you should consider more expensive repair work.

Clean the door handles of the house. They're very important, as they are something that buyers typically look at closely. (By the way, sometimes it's much easier to replace the door handles and other brass work on the front of the house than to polish it up.)

## Day 5: Clean the Back and Sides

You don't need to replicate the Palace of Versailles in your back-yard, but it should be neat and trim. Mow and pull the weeds.

And to make it look more livable, lots of fresh blooming flowers help. These can be purchased for very little and usually planted with ease. (Do the same for your side yards.)

If you have a patio, make sure it's free of clutter. A nice table and chairs helps. Toys, boxes, and other junk scattered around does not. If you don't have a patio, don't worry about it. It shouldn't detract that much from your home. Just be sure your lawn (if you have one) is well trimmed, with some lawn furniture on it.

## Day 6: Paint Inside, Especially the Kitchen

Paint all rooms where the existing paint is faded, peeling, scratched, marked, or otherwise looks bad.

If there's one room to work hardest on, it's the kitchen. For shaping up your house to get a quick sale, however, you can easily and inexpensively paint your kitchen. This should include the walls and ceiling. (In some cases with older cabinets that are in good physical shape, they too can be painted or restained.) The fresh coat of paint, particularly if it's white or a very light color, will freshen your kitchen no matter the condition of the cabinets, countertop, and appliances.

The kitchen is probably the single most important room of the house, in terms of buyer's perceptions. A modern, clean kitchen is a highlight. A dirty, old-fashioned kitchen will detract from a home's value.

**TIP**

The only way to really improve a kitchen is to fully renovate it. This is something that you may want to consider if yours is over 10 years old. However, major kitchen renovations can be very expensive. If you are thinking about a major kitchen renovation, then be sure you check out the cost/benefit of it. It may turn out that it would cost you more to do the work than you could get back in return on selling.

## Day 7: Paint the Guest Bathroom

Bathrooms are small. But just because they don't take up a lot of room doesn't mean they are easy to paint. Actually, their small size makes them more difficult.

The guest bathroom is something that buyers will always check. Doing a full renovation (replacing cabinets, tile, sink, tub, shower and so on) is very costly, but a simple repainting will refresh the room remarkably.

Be sure to choose light colored, glossy paints. Allow a full day for this.

## Day 8: Paint the Master Bathroom

As with the guest bathroom, the master bathroom is likewise important to buyers. Take a day to paint it. (Be sure not to get any paint on the fixtures or floor!)

## Day 9: Paint (or Clean) the Entry and the Living Areas

Be judicious here. Go through the house and look at your walls in the living areas. Are they scratched? Do they have marks? Do they look tired and worn?

If so, clean them up. If you've repainted in the previous six months, you may be able to clean them. Otherwise, plan on painting.

If the walls are already light and neutral, try using the same color. It will make it far easier to repaint.

**TIP**

Usually, ceilings remain clean, so you don't need to paint them. Just be very careful to not get any paint from the walls on the ceiling, or else you'll have to do the ceilings too, to match things out.

## Day 10: Paint (or Clean) the Bedrooms

The same applies here as it did to the living areas. You don't want to see marks, gashes, or scratches. And the easiest way to remove these is to repaint.

**TRAP**

Cleaning a spot on a wall seems a whole lot easier than painting the whole wall. However, when you clean a spot, you often only make it worse. The reason is that the cleaned area (assuming you can get the spot off), now makes the rest of the wall look dirty. Simply repainting the entire wall is usually easier.

If you're doing it yourself, be sure to remove as much furniture as possible. And use copious drop cloths to protect that which you can't move.

## Day 11: Wash the Windows

Dirty windows suggest a dirty house. And buyers always look out of (or sometimes into) the windows. If you don't do windows, hire someone who does. It won't cost much, and it will make a big difference.

## Day 12: Add Light

Clean all light fixtures. These accumulate lots of dirt and dead bugs over time. Cleaning them will increase their brightness and make your house look cheery.

You may want to replace existing light fixtures with brighter, more modern ones. This can quickly add a modern touch to your home. And more lighting gets rid of those dark, dismal corners that turn off buyers.

## Day 13: Remove Furniture

What you see as "cozy" furniture, most buyers will probably see as cluttered. Get a real estate agent, interior decorator, or stager to come in and help you evaluate your clutter. Most can quickly tell you what furniture to clean out to make your house look more open and friendly.

Then do it! Store it, sell it, dump it! Do so and buyers will think your home is just right.

When you're thinning out your furniture, here's a list to help you along:

### Clutter Removal Checklist

- Remove extra furniture. One double or queen in a bedroom should be the maximum. One table and set of chairs in a dining room. No cluttered chairs or couches in living or family room. No rugs on top of rugs.

- Remove any clothes that are not in drawers or *neatly* hung in closets. Most of us have too many clothes in our closets, which makes them look small. \_\_\_\_\_
- Remove any toys scattered on the floor and not neatly put away in drawers or boxes. \_\_\_\_\_
- Remove any items that would get in the way of a buyer's appreciation of your house. \_\_\_\_\_

## Day 14: Clean Inside

Work inside last. That way, if you spill something on it, you won't have to clean it a second time!

It should go without saying that you'll want to clean everywhere inside the house.

Spend a lot of time in the kitchen and bathrooms. Make sure that the counters are empty and that they are spotless. If you have tile, work a bit on getting the grout clean. Dress up the kitchen and bathroom cabinets.

Pay special attention to kitchen and bathroom floors. If your home is 25 years old or older, and has the original kitchen flooring, you may find that it's a darker color of yellow, green, or red. This was considered fashionable back then.

Today, however, kitchen floors tend to be either very light or very dark (black). The flooring color of your kitchen may severely date it.

While replacing cabinets, countertops, and appliances is usually very costly and can be a burden if you're still living in the home, replacing a kitchen floor with modern linoleum can be done in a single day and can be done relatively inexpensively. As with painting, this will immensely improve your kitchen's appearance, and if you choose carefully, it won't cost you an arm or a leg.

Also, clean the carpets. Buyers always look down as they walk through the home. Dirty carpets are a turnoff. (If you can afford it, replace the existing carpeting with inexpensive new carpeting. It will look great and make a terrific presentation.)

**TIP**

Clean inside early, but clean the carpet last. That way anything you spill will get cleaned up in the course of your work.

## Remember, First Impressions Count

If the would-be buyer's first impression is positive, then he or she walks through your home looking for reasons to seal the deal. If it's negative, that person goes through your home looking for reasons to avoid buying your property. You want to accent the positive and avoid the negative.

Following through on this 14-day shape-up will help guarantee a good first impression.

## After the 14-Day Shape-Up

Beyond the 14-day shape-up, what if your home needs additional work? What if it needs renovation?

Now you have to make the decision, "Is it worth it?" Keep in mind that if you don't do needed repair work, buyers will begin characterizing your property as a "fixer-upper" and will submit lowball offers. Buyers always exaggerate the cost of fixing up a property. On the other hand, we're probably talking serious money—tens of thousands of dollars—when it comes to major renovation.

Do a cost/reward analysis. How much will it cost to do the renovation work you anticipate? How much will it add to the value of your home? If it adds more value than it costs, borrow the money and do the work. If it doesn't, consider doing less work. Also, take into consideration the time to find a buyer. Sometimes doing the renovation, although it can take weeks or a month, means a much quicker sale.

The following list describes the most common major renovations, as well as tips on how to handle them.

## Most Common Renovation Work

- **Roof.** If you can simply fix an old roof where it's leaking and not replace it, do it. The cost is far, far less.
- **Insulation.** Older homes do not have much insulation, but today's buyers are keen on energy efficiency and will sometimes turn down a property because it lacks adequate insulation. The cost for adding blown-in insulation to an attic is low. To add insulation to walls on an already constructed house, however, is enormously costly and should be avoided if at all possible.
- **Electrical and plumbing.** Unless you sell "as is," you'll need to bring electricity and pipes up to minimal health and safety standards. (Selling "as is" almost always results in a lower price.) In most cases, the work needed to be done is minimal. On the other hand, if you have to convert galvanized steel pipes to copper pipes, be prepared for a major blow to your wallet. Be sure that all work involving safety—such as electrical, gas, heating, and so on—is done professionally, to avoid liability issues.
- **Walls.** External stucco should be patched, unless it's so badly broken up that it has to be totally replaced. Patching is cheap; replacement is very expensive. Interior wallboard should be patched where there are holes. You can do this yourself for next to nothing.

- **Garage door.** New hinges and springs are a good idea for safety reasons, and are inexpensive. Most wooden doors can be repaired inexpensively. Metal doors may have to be replaced.
- **Major landscaping.** If you put in a new lawn by sod, it costs more, but is instantly green. Seeds take up to three months to produce lush grass, but cost pennies per foot. Forget about adding shade trees. They need years to grow, and planting already large trees is costly. Flower beds, however, are inexpensive and almost immediately add color and vitality to landscaping. Also, fix the fence if it's falling down. Buyers start adding up costs when they see a broken fence.
- **Built-in appliances.** Broken appliances should be fixed or replaced. Sometimes it's cheaper to replace than to fix. For example, an entire electric range and oven may cost under $400, while a single burner (there are usually five to seven on the unit, including the oven) could cost $100.

There could, of course, be other areas requiring major repair. In all cases, you should get bids and competitively price materials yourself. This will determine whether you'll get your money for repair work out from the sale and/or whether doing so will help you sell faster.

## What If Your Property Is a Real Dog?

Many people have never seen a house in truly terrible condition. Typically, it results from a bad foreclosure where the old owners, upset about losing their property, take it out on the home. Needless to say, a house with the following really bad problems may not sell at all, or if it does, will command a greatly reduced price. (You may have picked this house up yourself at a bargain basement price as an investment.)

## Common Problems with a House in Really Bad Condition

Appliances. Ripped apart, stolen, or smashed

Bathroom fixtures. Broken and ripped from walls or out of floors

Light fixtures. Stolen or smashed (including the electrical receptacle)

Windows. Broken

Doors. Broken

Screens. Gone

Plumbing. Broken lines

Electrical. Main circuit box smashed, circuit breakers broken, wiring pulled out

Walls and ceiling. Major holes

Yard. No landscaping; weeds, rocks, and dirt

Fences. Broken

Exterior. Stucco falling apart, wood torn off or scratched, metal siding bent or broken loose

Ridiculous, you say? A house could never get that bad? I've seen them that bad and worse. But being in terrible shape doesn't mean the house is valueless. The condition just means that you have to decide on a plan of action.

## Options for a House in Terrible Shape

1. Fix it up completely.
2. Fix it up for safety and cosmetic effect.
3. Let it alone and sell it "as is" for much less.

At this point you have to realize that buyers ordinarily suffer from an appalling lack of imagination. If you have a house that is a real dog and you're fortunate enough to get a buyer to walk into the front door, chances are 99 out of 100 that the buyer will immediately turn around and walk out. The vast majority of buyers, even investor/buyers, won't want to fool around with a real dog *even if the price is cut-rate.*

That means that in order to sell the property, you're probably going to have to do some work. You fix it up either totally or just cosmetically enough to sell.

**TIP**

It can cost big bucks to fix up a house, so you should consider short-term financing in the form of a homeowner's loan or a home equity loan. In many cases, the interest on such a loan is tax deductible, as are *many* of your fix-up expenses. Check with your accountant.

## Do You Have the Energy?

Then there's the matter of how much energy you are willing (or have) to devote to the fix-up. Some of us are natural putterers. Fixing up a place is fun for us.

For most of us, however, fun is playing golf, watching TV, or reading a good book. And then there are those who have two left hands and who wouldn't think of trying to do a fix-up themselves.

Where do you fit in? (It's important to know, because if you have to hire everything out, it could be prohibitively expensive.)

Here's my suggestion. If you don't want to (or can't) spend a lot of energy yourself fixing up your home before you sell, forget it. Pay someone else to do what's minimally necessary to cosmetically clean and paint your property. Then take the lower price and wait the longer time to find a buyer. (Sometimes it's more important to cater to yourself than to cater to your house.)

On the other hand, if you're a bundle of energy, then by all means leap into the fray and fix up your house yourself. Try to do much of the work yourself, since that's actually the best way to save money.

Many sellers fall into the trap of thinking that by doing *excessive* fix-up work on their house they can make *even more* money from the sale. They overdo it. Keep in mind that your property will have a top market value beyond which it just won't exceed, at least not at the present time. When you fix it up, try to present it in such a way as to get that top dollar. Do the *minimal amount of fix-up possible.* Any additional fixing up could turn your property into a white elephant, overbuilt for its neighborhood.

# What to Do If You're "Underwater"

The real estate crisis that started in 2007 resulted in something like 9 million homeowners being "underwater." The term loosely means that you owe more on your home than it's worth. (Perhaps you remember the older term "upside down," which essentially meant the same thing.)

Being underwater can affect you in a variety of ways, depending on your financial situation:

- **If you can afford your monthly payment,** being underwater means that you have a paper loss. Your house has lost all its value *on paper*. However, if you sit tight and keep making those payments, eventually (though it may take years) the market will come back and you'll once again have equity— you'll eventually get above water.

- **If you can't afford your monthly payment** because it was too high to begin with or because it reset to a much higher rate, your situation, as you probably realize, is far more dire. Your two best alternatives would normally be to resell or refinance—to get out from under. But neither may be possible when you owe more than your home is worth. Therefore, you might soon be facing foreclosure (see the next chapter).

Many of those reading this are in the second category—facing a mortgage payment that's too high, yet finding it near impossible to refinance or to resell. In this chapter we're going to look at just what you can do to save your credit and, in some cases, save your house.

## Understand the True Nature of Your Situation

As noted earlier, you're not alone. Millions of homeowners are in a similar fix.

Further, the situation is probably not of your making—at least not entirely. Many, if not most, of those who obtained mortgages that reset to much higher interest and payment levels did not understand the true nature of the financing. Some were told that when the mortgage reset, they could easily refinance out of it. Others did not understand that the mortgage would reset.

To make it all worse, almost no one foresaw the deep slide in home prices that occurred starting in 2007 and the enormous number of foreclosures that deepened and lengthened that slide. Most people predicted a housing market that, if not going up at the rapid pace of 2001–2006, would at least stabilize. They anticipated that as a worst-case scenario, they would have enough equity to resell, even if not at a profit. They never foresaw falling prices, foreclosures, and few sales.

## What Can You Do?

If you're underwater—can't make your payments—and do nothing, it could actually get worse. As long as you can make your housing payments, your situation is stable. The lender won't take your house away no matter what the value falls to.

On the other hand, if you can't and don't make your payments, your situation is in motion. It's only a matter of time until you face foreclosure and the loss of your property.

As this is written, there are literally millions of former homeowners who either have lost or are in the process of losing their homes. Some are renting, some have moved in with relatives, and some are literally out on the street.

But that need not necessarily happen to you. For the remainder of this chapter, we'll look into your options when you're underwater and can't make your payments. Before we start, however, let's consider that final option that many homeowners feel they have in the back of their minds—the atomic bomb of ownership—simply walking away from the mortgage and the property.

## Should You "Walk"?

No one is putting handcuffs on you. If you don't like your housing situation, you can simply walk away from it. You won't be put in jail (unless there was fraud involved when you obtained the mortgage).

**TRAP**

During the real estate meltdown that began in 2007, more people "walked" away from their properties than at any time since the Great Depression of the 1930s.

However, don't entertain the misconception that there won't be consequences. When a property owner walks, here are some of the potentially severe results:

### Consequences of "Walking"

- You'll lose any and all interest you may have in your home. If there's any equity left, it will evaporate.
- The lender will almost certainly foreclose. It will inform credit bureaus that you did not make your payments and, eventually, that it foreclosed on you and you lost your home.
- Having a foreclosure will remain on your credit record for years, in some cases decades. It will mean that any new mortgage lender will think twice before giving you a new mortgage. In other words, you'll find it more difficult to buy another property—but not impossible (see Chapter 9 on seller financing).
- Your ability to get other credit, including credit cards and personal loans, could be adversely affected.
- You may even have trouble renting another home. Most landlords today require a credit report, and when it shows late payments and a foreclosure, they may be reluctant to rent to you.
- In some cases, the lender may actually come after you for any money it loses because you walked! (See next Trap.)

In short, walking will not be a piece of cake. It should only be considered as a last alternative. But should it be considered an alternative at all?

**TRAP**

In some cases where lenders foreclose judicially, they may be able to obtain a deficiency judgment against you, garnish your salary, and attach your assets to recover any losses they sustain in foreclosing on your underwater property. Be sure to check with a good attorney before letting your property go to foreclosure.

**TIP**

In those states which have "purchase money" laws, deficiency judgments may not be allowed if the loan in foreclosure was used to originally purchase your home.

My feeling is that you should never consider walking without first consulting a financial coach—someone to whom you can tell your entire story. This person should have a strong financial background and be able to make sound money recommendations to you. In some unusual cases, walking may make sense.

## Talk to Your Lender

Often those who talk to their lenders find that a work-out of some sort can be arranged. After all, chances are your lender has had to handle dozens—if not hundreds or even thousands—of foreclosures. The last thing it needs or wants is another.

Therefore, if you talk to your lender, you may be able to work out an arrangement that will work for both of you.

The federal government has been leaning on lenders to try and work things out with borrowers who are having trouble making payments. However, with so many borrowers in default, most lenders are overwhelmed and simply don't have the staff to contact everyone, or even most borrowers.

Here's a list of things you will want to discuss with your lender:

### Things to Discuss with Your Lender

- **Reduce your monthly payments.** This can be done—either temporarily or permanently—by extending the term of your loan, reducing the interest rate, or adding some of the interest not paid to the mortgage principal.
- **Forgive your back payments.** The lender has the power to simply write off the payments for which you are in arrears. It can do the same for penalties and additional interest.
- **Reduce the loan balance.** If you're underwater, it means that your mortgage is higher than the home's value. The lender, with the swish of a pen and the printing of some

documents, can cut the loan balance to below the home's value. This will have the effect of lowering your monthly payments. Most lenders, however, will not do this unless pressured. (See "short sales," below.)

- **Temporarily stop all payments.** The lender has the power to halt your payments for a few months or longer while you get on your feet. (For example, if you've been ill or laid off and can't make the payments.) The interest left unpaid can be added to the mortgage or simply forgiven.

- **Anything else that will get you current and save your home.** Lenders can be creative when they're highly motivated.

## Finding Someone to Talk To

Often the hardest part of talking to your lender is finding someone there. Your lender may or may not have a local office. It could be across the country.

Or it may turn out that the lender to whom you're making your payments isn't actually the lender who owns your loan. Rather, your contact is only a servicer, a company that collects payments and manages your loan. It may or may not have the power to make changes that you need.

Or your lender may not have anyone available to talk with you. It may be so overwhelmed with defaulting mortgages and foreclosures that it can't give you an appointment with a loan officer within a reasonable period of time—say a month.

Or it may give you someone to talk to, but, that person is only a secretary and can only relay what you say to someone else who is not available . . . and won't be available to you to make a decision.

In short, getting to the right person with whom to talk about your mortgage can be half (or more than half!) of the battle. How do you do it?

The only answer I have seen that works is persistence. It's a fact that the squeaky wheel gets the grease. Start with whomever you normally make your mortgage payment to and work your way upward until you finally get to someone in authority. Then bug them, or their secretary, or whomever else you can reach—including the CFO and CEO of the lending institution!—until you get their attention.

Don't stop until you get a reasonably timed (within a week) appointment to see them. And then go there. (If it's a lender across the country, they will almost always designate a local rep, once they finally agree to talk with you.)

## What to Do When You Finally Meet a Loan Officer Face-to-Face

Be prepared. You need to:

- Know exactly where you stand currently with your mortgage.
- Have your "demands" in order: Do you want the lender to restructure your loan? Do you want forgiveness of back payments? Do you want the lender to write off a portion of the mortgage, if you sell?
- Be prepared to compromise: Are you willing to sell your property to get out from under?
- Be prepared to pressure the lender.

Let's talk a bit about this last one. Most times, lenders are more than willing to add back payments to the mortgage balance. But, ask them to write off some of that mortgage and they get apoplectic. How do you get a lender to bite the bullet and take the big step that may be necessary to get you off the hook?

## How Do You Pressure the Lender?

In the final analysis, it all comes down to trade-offs. From the lender's perspective, what can it do to minimize any loss on your property? If you can show the lender a way to minimize its losses—a way out—you've probably got a deal.

**TRAP**

Some lenders simply aren't sane, in the financial sense. You expect them to act in their own best interests to minimize loss and maximize gain, but some simply will do the opposite. If that's the case, then talking to them may not do much good at all.

I suggest you go with a triple-barreled approach. For the first barrel, you want the lender to reduce your mortgage payments to something you can afford over time, but you realize at the outset that it's going to be a tough sell. Your payments may have reset to as much as twice what you were originally paying. To bring them back to your old payment, the lender would have to restructure your mortgage by cutting the interest rate almost in half. Not impossible, but unlikely.

Your second barrel is a refinance. If the lender won't cut your interest rate, perhaps it will refinance your home with a new low-rate teaser similar to the one you may have originally had. This will cut your payments at least for a few years, which will give you a breather.

Again, not impossible, but unlikely if the value of your property has fallen since the original mortgage was made and you've been told by mortgage brokers that you simply don't have enough equity to warrant a new loan. Besides, this lender probably would like to be rid of the property, not to refinance it into another long term loan.

Finally, your last barrel is that you're willing to sell your home to get out from under the mortgage. Indeed, you may feel you can find a buyer . . . at market value. But, because of falling prices, this is below what you owe. (You are, after all, underwater.) Therefore, you want the lender to be willing to accept a "short" (less than is owed) payoff to make the deal.

Again, most lenders simply don't want to consider this. It means writing off a portion of their mortgage—showing a loss. Do this too many times and the lending officer could lose his job, and the lender itself could become insolvent.

Nevertheless, as we'll see, this last barrel, surprisingly, could be your best bet.

## Your Ammunition

Why would a lender do a major restructuring of your loan, or refinance it, or contemplate a short sale? Consider:

As it now stands, you're probably months behind on your payments. The lender may or may not have already started the foreclosure process by recording a Notice of Default.

Depending on which state you live in, it could take months, or as long as a year, to foreclose and take the property away from you. During that time the following is likely to happen:

### From the Lender's Perspective

- You won't make payments, so the loan will remain "nonperforming" with the lender losing interest.
- You won't maintain the property. After all you're going to lose it, so why make costly repairs?
- You'll likely move out, meaning that the property could be subject to vandalism.
- After the lender takes the property back, it will cost plenty of dough to refurbish it.

- When it comes back on the market as lender owned (technically called REO—Real Estate Owned), it will need to pay a commission to an agent to facilitate a sale.
- When the lender takes a property back on a nonperforming loan, the federal government often insists it beef up its reserves in anticipation of a loss. This is a drain on the lender's capital.
- It still may not be able to sell as an REO for months or longer, and all the while the lender is continuing to lose interest. When it sells, it very well might take a big loss on the property.

In short, once you see things from the lender's perspective, your position suddenly has possibilities. The lender may actually be in more hot water than you! And, there's lots of ways you can help the lender save money:

1. You can get the loan back to performing, if only the lender will restructure it—write down some of the principal, reduce the interest rate, and lower the payments. This is the easiest and simplest method, if the lender sees reason.

2. You can get the loan paid off, if only the lender will refinance it to something you can afford. The drawback here is that the lender still has a loan on the property, something it probably doesn't want.

3. You can get the loan (and the property) completely out of the lender's hair if it will accept less than is owed in a short sale.

So, when you see the lender and explain how doing a restructure, a refinance, or a short sale will help matters, what's likely to happen?

A lot depends on how underwater you are. If you're only behind a few payments and if the mortgage is close to the market value, the lender may go with a restructure or a refinance. It's the sensible thing to do.

However, in my experience, the lender who will neither restructure nor refinance may say something like, "Yes, we'll consider a short sale. Find a buyer."

It's not exactly a great commitment, but, it is enough to get you going.

Now price your house to sell, even if it's less than you owe. Get it listed and agree to pay the lowest commission (see Chapter 3 on getting an agent). Find a buyer, and when you do, write up a sales agreement for less than you owe, contingent on getting a short payoff from the lender.

**TIP**

Today, most buyers are well aware of what a short sale/short payoff is and will be willing to go along with you, particularly once you explain you've already spoken to the lender who's tentatively agreed.

Now, go back to the lender and present your deal. (It should be easier to get in, once you've already found someone to talk to.)

As I said, if the lender is financially sane and if you are selling your home at market, the lender should accept. (The great problem will be time. As noted, lenders are themselves awash with foreclosures and getting them to act can require the patience of Job.)

Get that lender's acceptance of your deal, however, and you're no longer underwater.

**NOTE**

Lenders report short sales to credit bureaus and they can adversely affect your credit, though usually not nearly as much as a foreclosure.

## Another Alternative: Rent the Home Out

Here's an idea that can work. When you can't restructure your existing loan or refinance to a new one, and instead of selling short or losing your home to foreclosure, why not try renting it out until times get better? After all, at some time in the future, your property is certainly going to be worth more than it is today. (Inflation alone will see to that!)

Why not rent until times improve?

Most sellers have three good reasons for not wanting to rent out their property:

First, they want to be done with it, one way or another. It's an emotional anchor to be continually worrying about the house, what's going to happen to it. Better, many sellers say, to have done with it even if that means foreclosure. (Bad answer—see the next chapter.)

Second, many sellers have never been landlords. They may feel they're jumping from the frying pan into the fire. What if the tenants don't pay? What if they move out and leave the place a mess? Worst of all, what if they don't pay, don't move, and still mess up the place?

Third, you may not be able to rent the home for enough money to pay for the PITI. (That stands for mortgage principal, interest, taxes, and insurance.) In other words, it will cost you money out of pocket each month to keep the place and rent it.

**TRAP**

While foreclosures are increasing, in many areas there's a shortage of rentals, and rental rates are going up. Don't think you can't rent your property for enough to cover expenses until you've checked it out with a property management company. You might be pleasantly surprised!

All of these reasons need to be considered. Just keep in mind, however, that while renting your home may be an inconvenience, it could be a way out.

Is it worth the emotional hassle of handling a rental to save your credit? Can you find good tenants who won't wreck the place? (I have, almost 100 percent of the time.) And with the tax write-offs that a rental provides, you just may come close to break-ing even, or actually make a profit! (See Chapter 11 for more details on this.)

In short, converting to a rental may be a better answer. Of course, you still need to come up with the money to make your mortgage current. And you'll have to find another place to live. But, where there's a will, there's a way.

# How to Stop Foreclosure

In the last chapter, we talked about what to do if you're underwater. That means that you owe more than your property's worth.

But what do you do when you're underwater, your lender has filed a Notice of Default (which starts the foreclosure process), and an auction of your property looms not far in the future. Maybe you only have a few months left, or a few weeks, or even just a few days! How do you stop the foreclosure process and save your home—at least so that you can sell it? (And in the process save some of your credit rating, if not your equity.)

Obviously, paying up any back payments (or if you are nearing an auction sale, refinancing the mortgage) will stop foreclosure. But, how do you get the money to do that?

Here are some of the things you may want to consider.

## 1. Talk to Your Lender Immediately, Today, Right Now!

It's like meeting a bully in an alleyway who looks like he wants to fight. You can "put up your dukes" or you can see if you can talk your way out of it.

The first thing I suggested in the preceding chapter was talking to the lender. If you didn't do it, now's the time. Demand to see your lender. Get in there. And find out if something can be done to at least slow down the foreclosure process.

Remember the tips from the last chapter:

1. Restructure the mortgage by cutting the interest rate or reducing the principal, thus getting lower payments.
2. Refinance to a new loan with lower payments, paying off the one in foreclosure.
3. Get the lender to consider a short payoff if you sell.

**TIP**

Talking to your adversary, whether a bully or a lender—some people would say there's not much difference!—transforms you from an object into a person. You've got a personality, warmth, humor, and value. In short, it's a lot harder to beat up on someone you know and like than on a complete stranger.

Remember, the lender has it within its power to slow down the foreclosure process. If you can come up with a viable alternative, the lender can delay the auction of your home from a few days to indefinitely. This isn't going to happen, however, until you've talked to that lender.

## 2. Consider a "Deed in Lieu of Foreclosure"

This is not the best of alternatives, but at least it will ultimately show that you cooperated to help the lender. Here, instead of waiting for the lender to go through the entire lengthy foreclosure process, you give the lender a deed to the property. In essence, you say, "You don't need to foreclose, Mr. Lender. I'm moving out and handing you the deed to my home, saving you time and money."

The lender gets the home, presumably, in good condition and then immediately attempts to resell it. Of course, you likely won't get any money out of this deal. But, at least you won't have a foreclosure on your credit report. And you've taken an honorable way out.

**TRAP**

Lenders now regularly report receiving a "deed in lieu" to credit agencies, and it's considered a bad mark against your credit. But, usually, it's not as bad as a foreclosure.

Note that in most cases you can't simply send a deed to the lender. You must negotiate this so that the lender accepts it.

## 3. Look into Bankruptcy

If this sounds like a desperate measure, it is. I'm not suggesting that you file a Chapter 13 bankruptcy simply to stop the foreclosure process. But it may be that by the time you're facing foreclosure, you may be in financial trouble across the board. If that's the case, then by all means you should check with your financial counselor and/or a good attorney.

Once you file for bankruptcy and your home is included as part of your personal property, the judge in the case may have the power to slow down the foreclosure process for many months. This could give you time to explore other alternatives such as refinancing or selling.

Keep in mind, however, that currently the judge does not have the power to restructure the loan—that is, he or she cannot reduce the principal, the interest, or the monthly payment. As of this writing, however, several bills are before Congress to give judges just this authority. You may want to check to see if any have passed by the time you read this.

## 4. Soldiers and Sailors Civil Relief Act (SSCRA)

This legislation was originally passed in 1918 to help servicemen during the First World War. It was rewritten in 1940 to help service members of the Second World War. And it was extended and expanded in 2003 for service members involved in the war in Iraq.

Today, SSCRA allows a court to stop foreclosure for the service person and dependents while they're on active duty and for up to three months afterward.

It applies to either a mortgage or a trust deed, and the obligation had to have originated prior to entry into military service. The property must be owned by a service member or his or her dependent at the time the relief is sought.

The relief that may be obtained includes a stay of the proceedings, diminished payments, or an extension of the maturity date of the mortgage.

If a foreclosure judgment has already been ordered or a sale made, the judgment may be reexamined and set aside, or the period of redemption extended.

It's important to understand that SSCRA does not relieve you of any obligations. It only delays or slows down the process.

If you think you might find benefit here, you should Google "SSCRA" to get more information.

## 5. Attack the Paperwork

The essence of a mortgage (or trust deed) for a lender is all of the paperwork. You may remember that when you obtained the loan, there were dozens, perhaps as many as a hundred pages of documents you had to sign. They all were carefully printed out. And if there were any errors, typically the entire page (if not the entire series of documents) had to be reprinted. You had to sign your legal name over and over again.

The reason, quite simply, is that if there were a mistake, it could invalidate the entire mortgage. That's right—one goof on the part of the lender and the whole loan could be kaput. Therefore, it could be worth your while to have the paperwork to your transaction carefully examined. (You should have saved it or the lender should provide copies.)

**TRAP**

Lenders are well aware of the need for accurate documents. That often includes several provisions that say that if there are any errors or omissions, you the borrower will cooperate by signing and making good on whatever was wrong or left out. It's unclear, however, just how much force such a provision has when you're in foreclosure and discover a lender snafu.

One of the more serious problems could occur over Regulation Z, the Truth in Lending document(s) that you are required to receive under RESPA (Real Estate Settlement Procedures Act). If you did not receive the appropriate paperwork, or it was incorrect, or not timely, you could use it to challenge the entire mortgage.

Attacking the paperwork is not an easy route to take. The lender will surely work aggressively to deny your claim. And you probably will have to go to court.

Nonetheless, it could very well be a way to stop foreclosure, *if* an error was made.

How often are errors made? I don't know of any statistics released to the public, but suffice to say that borrowers rarely challenge lenders here. My own experience with lenders is that they make far more mistakes than they would like anyone to believe.

## 6. Try Refinancing with a Private Lender

If you can't get an institutional lender to refinance your home, you may want to consider a private lender. Remember, if you refinance, you may get enough money to pay off your mortgage and thereby stop foreclosure, assuming you do it before time runs out on your redemption period.

Private lenders are exactly what the term means. They are individuals, or sometimes small corporations, that offer mortgage financing . . . at a price. That price usually has much higher interest rates. And, because they often want higher LTVs (Loan-to-Value ratios), it may not always be possible to use their services.

But some private lenders will consider your other assets (car, boat, motorcycle, stocks, and so on) in the loan. That could increase the amount they will consider lending you.

The important thing to remember is that private lenders can structure a mortgage to fit your needs. For example, they may offer a reduced payment for three to five years—a long teaser. Or they might offer no payments at all for a few years and then a balloon payment for the entire balance. (You'd have to then refinance or resell to make the payoff.)

In short, it's worth the time to check with a few private lenders to see if they can provide relief. Since most are small, local lenders, you'll need to find them in your state. Google "Private mortgage lenders." Just be sure they are located in your state, since most may not be licensed to make out of state loans.

## Always Protect Your Credit

**TRAP**

The lender's belief: A borrower who learns to live with one foreclosure can live with many more.

If you ever hope to buy another house in the future, do everything you can to protect your mortgage credit. Try to find a way to pay off the mortgage. Get yourself off the hook.

Don't think you can sneak by a lender. Every mortgage loan application asks if you have *ever* had a foreclosure. Most, today, also ask if you have ever given a deed in lieu of foreclosure. (If you fudge on the application, the foreclosure could show up on a credit report. Even if it doesn't show up and you do get the loan, should you later default and it turns out that you lied on your application, you could be liable for serious civil and/or criminal penalties.)

**TRAP**

Unless you obtained the mortgage as part of the purchase price (and only in those states which have "purchase money mortgage" laws), even if you walk, the lender could go to court and obtain a deficiency judgment against you for any money it loses by taking the property. This judgment would follow you.

## Avoid the Mortgage Credit Trap

In many cases, it is possible to avoid foreclosure. It may not be easy. You may need to change your plans or take actions you'd rather avoid. You will almost certainly need to become actively involved with your lender.

You may even have to sell an item you love, like a boat or car, to raise money for mortgage payments. You may have to do things you disdain, like borrowing from relatives. But where there's a will there's a way. And this is one case where finding the way will bring you a much happier future.

Being in foreclosure is acutely unpleasant. But don't give up hope. If you can just hang on long enough, things usually turn around.

# Selling Faster "By Owner"

Ask any seller what is the biggest expense in selling his or her home, and he or she will say, "The real estate agent's commission."

Today's commissions typically range from 4 to 6 percent, depending on the area of the country, the difficulty in selling the property, and the negotiating skill of the seller. On a home that sells for $200,000 (close to the national median price), that's between $8,000 and $12,000. I don't think there's ever been a seller who hasn't wished he or she could avoid paying out that much money. And some sellers do avoid it, by selling on their own.

Each year, about 10 to 15 percent of homes are sold "by owner" without going through an agent. These sellers either save money on the commission they would otherwise pay or get a faster sale by lowering their price—or both. You can be among their number.

However, selling FSBO (For Sale By Owner) takes a certain mindset that not everyone has. It also takes patience and effort. It would be a mistake to think that all you need do is put a sign in the front yard and wait for buyers to hand you a deposit and a sales contract. To sell FSBO, you're going to have to do some of the work that an agent does. Of course, the results can be quite rewarding.

In this chapter, we're going to see what's involved in a FSBO sale and how to get started pulling it off successfully.

## Can You Sell "By Owner" in Today's Market?

The common wisdom is that FSBOs are most easily done in strong markets. Most people believe that if you're in a hot—or sellers'—market, your chances of selling by owner are dramatically increased. After all, if there are more buyers than sellers, it only stands to reason that it's easier to make a sale and save a commission.

However, FSBOs also do well in very weak markets. Statistically, just about as many are sold when the market's down as when it's up. So it really doesn't make a whole lot of difference what the market's doing. Your chances of selling by owner remain about the same.

## Can You Really Do It?

If you have never sold a home through an agent, then I would discourage you from trying to sell on your own the first time out. Just as with doing your own taxes, it's better if you have an expert do it at least the first time. That way, you can see how a deal is handled and get a feel for the steps involved. That doesn't mean that you can't do it yourself the first time you sell. It just means that the chances of your getting yourself in trouble or ruining what otherwise would be a good deal are too great to warrant the attempt.

### Dealing with Buyers

If you've bought and sold a couple of homes, you may decide to move forward on your own. If you do, keep in mind that you will be on the front line in dealing with buyers. Yes, we're all people, and buyers are just nice people looking for a home. But the moment they become potential buyers for your home, they also become adversaries.

Their goals are exactly the opposite of yours. They are trying to get the price down; you want to keep it up. They want you to throw in the refrigerator, the furniture, maybe even the cat. You want to take everything with you. They want you to finance the house at 3 percent interest. You want them to get their own loan or pay you 20 percent interest.

When dealing with buyers, you're going to have to be prepared to tackle an often aggressive adversary, all the while putting on a smile and keeping a cheerful outlook. The buyers are going to make you sweat, make you worry, even make you fearful. Are you ready to cope with that?

## Who Will Handle the Paperwork?

Many owners feel that one of the biggest obstacles to selling by owner is the paperwork. In addition to the deposit, there are disclosures to deal with, escrow documents, deeds, and a host of other items. Professionals such as agents and attorneys are trained to deal with these on a regular basis and know their ins and outs. You, however, who may only sell a home once a decade, can find the paperwork arcane, difficult, and potentially dangerous from a legal perspective. Is there some way for you to safely deal with it?

The answer is, yes. Today you can hire an attorney and/or (in some cases) an agent on a fee basis—or a reduced commission basis—to do the paperwork for you.

My suggestion is that unless you are very competent in real estate yourself, don't even attempt to draw up a sales agreement or handle any other documents. The chances of your getting into legal hot water are too great. Plan on spending what it takes (usually not that much) to have a professional handle it for you.

Most of the FSBO Web sites offer lists of professionals that will work for you on a fee basis. Here are several to check out:

www.owners.com
www.fsbo.com
www.forsalebyowner.com

**TRAP**

When you hire an attorney, be sure that he or she is a *real estate* specialist. Most attorneys aren't, and they can muck up a deal by knowing enough *generally* but not enough *specifically* about how to handle the transaction.

## Do You Have the Time to Sell "By Owner"?

Buyers don't do anything for your convenience. They do everything for their own. They figure that if they're going to spend $200,000, more or less, on a house, then you, the seller, had better cater to them. That means that you have to be ready to show the place at the drop of hat. A couple drives by, sees your home, and calls. But, you tell them, you haven't dressed, you haven't cleaned the house, and you've got a terrible headache.

Okay, they say, there are other houses to see and plenty of agents who'll show them. *Damn*, you think, and let them in. Are you prepared for that? (Keep in mind that you have to be prepared to show your property at a moment's notice even if you work through an agent!)

## What If Potential Buyers Ask You About Financing?

Today that's easy. You don't have to deal with the buyers delicate questions about their financing, which was just what you had to do in the past.

Today, just tell the buyer to contact a good mortgage broker. You can even call several in advance and line them up.

Mortgage brokers are key here. They will talk with buyers, find out about their financial situation, and even provide you with a letter of approval stating how much money they can pay each month and how big a mortgage they can afford.

If you don't know a good mortgage broker, ask a real estate agent to refer you to one. (It doesn't have to be *your* agent—they will be happy to help in the hope of eventually getting your listing.) Ask friends, relatives, or associates for good references. As a last resort, you can always check the Yellow Pages or go online, where there are hundreds!

## What About Marketing?

When you sell by yourself, you must do everything in your power to let people know your home is for sale. That includes putting your property on the MLS (Multiple Listing Service).

The MLS is what agents use to market properties. Virtually all the agents in your area will belong and will see what's listed there.

Of course, you personally can't put your property on the MLS, at least not as of this writing. Instead, it must be done by a Realtor member. In the past this meant listing.

## Flat Fee MLS

However, today there's the "Flat Fee MLS." Here, for a flat fee typically under $400, a member agent will list your home on the MLS. Then all the other agents in the area can see it's for sale . . . and work on it.

It's important to understand what you get . . . and what you don't get with a Flat Fee MLS.

### What You Get with a Flat Fee MLS

- Your property gets listed on the MLS.
- Typically, it will be picked up and shown on www.realtor.com, which is the most widely viewed home buyers' site.
- Often it will be repeated by such other Web sites as www.yahoo.com or www.aol.com.
- You get the opportunity to tell a buyer's agent (as part of the listing) how big a commission you'll pay. It's typically between 2 and 3 percent.

### What You Don't Get with a Flat Fee MLS

- You don't get any help in selling the property from the lister. The flat fee typically allows you access to the MLS, that's all. The lister won't show, negotiate, or do any paperwork . . . unless you pay an additional fee.

It's important to understand the difference between the *listing* agent and the *buyer's* agent. The listing agent is the one who works for you and who normally performs all the services of selling your home noted above. The buyer's agent procures the buyers and typically works for them.

You're paying the listing agent under $400 here. However, you want to pay a reasonable commission to the buyer's agents to get them to work on the listing. That's why I suggest offering between 2 and 3 percent or what's typically half a normal full commission.

**NOTE** While the buyer's agent usually represents the buyer, he or she can also technically represent you—see Chapter 3.

**TRAP**

If you don't offer a commission to the buyer's agents, how many of them do you think are going to be eager to work at selling your home?

Flat Fee MLS listings are available from most FSBO Web sites, including those listed earlier.

## Listing Online

Virtually all of the online FSBO sites accept listings. You can put up images of your property, fully describe it, and talk about schools, shopping, transportation, and more.

Owners.com, as of this writing, offers a basic free listing service and advanced listings for a nominal fee. These include multiple images, a telephone answering service, signs, flyers, and a host of other aids including (as noted earlier) sources for professionals such as mortgage brokers and attorneys who may be able to help you.

One of the great advantages of listing online is that it provides a neutral location where potential buyers can check out all of the features of your home. An ad or a phone call can direct them to your site. From there they can learn virtually everything they'll need to know to help them make a purchase decision about your home. Then, when they finally do see it, they are (hopefully!) primed and ready to buy.

## Flyers

Creating flyers and giving them to neighbors (and making them available in a little box on your sign) will help. So will putting up notices on bulletin boards, contacting any nearby housing offices of major companies, and even going online and leaving messages on electronic bulletin boards.

Be sure the flyer includes a photo of your house—one view of the front, another inside—and a list of all its features. The flyers, which should include a map showing exactly where your house is located, can be run off at a local copy shop. Be sure your name and phone number are prominently displayed.

Give everyone who comes by your home a copy. A buyer may want to come back later and not be able to find the property, or may want to call you and not have your phone number. This is an excellent way for a buyer to recall both.

## Newspaper Ads

Of course, newspaper advertising is a must. Here are some tips on that most expensive of venues.

In newspaper advertising (as elsewhere), less is more. The classic mistake that novice sellers make is saying too much in the ad (and paying too much for it as well). I've seen sellers take out full-column, even double-column, ads for their home—unnecessarily spending hundreds of dollars. Perhaps they are hoping to compete with agents' ads.

One of the biggest misunderstandings that all sellers have is to think that a buyer who sees their ad in the paper is likely to come right out and buy their house. Buyers rarely buy homes they see advertised. Real estate agents put ads in the paper for two reasons: to appease sellers by appearing to work hard—and to get listings!

Agents know that callers on ads often have their own property to sell. They hope to sign them up. An FSBO seller, on the other hand, has only one home to sell. You can't sign up a listing, and most of the time the buyers who come over will think your home doesn't match their desires and won't buy. You just have to hope to hit big enough numbers to eventually catch a live one.

Don't get discouraged, play the odds. Get enough potential buyers to read your ad and come through that front door, and one of them will make an offer.

Of course, agents are competing with you, trying to lure in buyers and sellers with their own advertising. Since they have many properties, and since most buyers gravitate to agents, the odds are in their favor.

Except for one thing: the words "By Owner."

Buyers love to check out FSBOs because they smell a bargain and know that agents aren't likely to show them these properties. Therefore, by writing "FSBO" (or "By Owner") at the top of your ad, you can be well on the way to attracting buyers.

### Creating Your "By Owner" Ad

1. Indicate you're selling FSBO or By Owner.
2. Give the style of the home and the neighborhood location (but not the address, for security reasons) and include any special features.
3. Give the number of bedrooms and baths in the house.
4. Give the price.
5. Give the general condition of the property.
6. Give one outstanding feature the property has.
7. Give your phone number as well as a Web site address. (For security reasons, it's probably wise not to advertise your location.)

Here's a typical ad from a newspaper:

**By Owner**
In Maple Schools
Large 4 bed, 3 bath,
Newly painted, pool, spa
Must sell $135,000    555-2134
www.owners.com/yourlistingpage

This newspaper ad is lean and mean. There are few extraneous words. And it cuts right to the chase with "must sell" and the price.

Presumably, any buyer interested in the price range, location, and schools will find the ad enticing—and will call.

Would a bigger ad be better? Many advertising specialists say bigger is better because it's easier to see. However, in the case of homes for sale, buyers are usually meticulous in scrutinizing long lists of tiny ads looking for bargains, so the cost of a big ad might just be wasted. In addition, a bigger ad might just show how inexperienced you really are at selling a home.

Finally, anything else you might add at this point could just as likely scare away as many buyers as it attracts. For example, you list that the home has a dog runway. There might be more buyers who don't have dogs—and don't want a dog run—than do.

If you still feel uncomfortable in designing an ad, check out your local library or bookstore. There are at least a dozen good books on designing advertising that gets results. Take one out and follow its advice.

## Get a Good Sign

A sign is a must. It doesn't have to be elaborate, but it should be large enough to be seen easily by motorists passing by and it should look good. You can find ready-made FSBO signs at stationery stores for just a few dollars, but I suggest popping for the $50 or so it costs to have one made up just for you. (Or get a professional sign from a Web site.) After all, you're talking about saving a commission worth thousands. Surely you can afford a few bucks for a sign!

When you get the sign, plant it firmly in the lawn, where it can most easily be seen by people passing in cars. This isn't necessarily in the center of your front yard. It could be off to the side or even attached to a tree or fence. Don't forget to put your phone number and Web address on the sign. Some sellers also add, "BY APPOINTMENT ONLY." That doesn't mean that a potential buyer won't come rapping at your door, but it tends to suggest to most that a call first might be in order. Most of all, don't forget the magic words, "By Owner!"

**TRAP**

Some locales have sign ordinances. These may restrict the number of signs you can use, their size, or even whether you're allowed to put a sign out at all. Check with your local building department or homeowners association if you have any questions here.

## What About Showing the Property?

That's up to you. After all, who else is there?

There are several concerns here, the biggest of which usually is security. You're letting people into your house without really knowing who they are or what their ulterior motives might be. You could be setting yourself up for a robbery . . . or worse.

For some sellers this is no problem—they just don't worry about it and take their chances. For others, it's a big concern. If it concerns you, forget selling FSBO and list your property with an agent who can screen people before he or she brings them by.

**TIP**

Some FSBO sellers concerned with security require potential buyers to call first and won't show the property until they get the buyer's full name, phone number, and address. Then they call the buyer back. At least that tends to confirm that buyers have their own place and are somewhat established. On the other hand, it can insult some buyers and cause them not to come by.

When you do show the property, warmly welcome the prospective buyers and point out the amenities of the house. After you've talked for a few moments, allow the buyers to wander through the property themselves. (They need to be able to feel that it's their own house.)

**TRAP**

You never know who's honest and who's not. Buyers wandering through might just slip a precious necklace or watch into their pocket and be gone. Therefore, put away all valuables before showing your house. (You should take the same precautions even if the house is listed with an agent.)

## Have a Guest Book

Have a guest book located conveniently near the front door. Ask potential buyers to sign their names and give their phone numbers. This gives you a record of who came through so you can call people back.

Later, if you subsequently list with an agent, you can exclude those people and need not pay a commission if they buy.

## Will You Need to "Open Escrow"?

What could be simpler? After a buyer has signed a sales agreement to purchase your home, just take the document down to a local escrow company. Any escrow company will take it from there.

But don't expect advice, or at least good advice, from every escrow officer. Escrow companies are neutral third parties. In most cases, they know their job fairly well. They'll prepare all the necessary documents to close the deal and they'll tell you what actions, documents, or monies have to be deposited to escrow in order to make the deal. But don't expect your escrow officer to answer questions such as, "Which termite inspection company should I use?" Or "The buyer wants me to repaint the interior, but I don't want to—how do we resolve this?" Those are problems you'll have to resolve yourself.

Keep in mind that very often the various people involved in the sale will provide the necessary information and direction to help with closing. The loan officer, for example, will often help the buyer straighten out credit problems. The real estate attorney will help you clear up title problems. The escrow officer may provide the document for a second mortgage, if you need it. And so forth.

In truth, in most cases, once you have found buyers who have signed a purchase agreement, the remainder of the transaction should progress smoothly. You should have few problems, assuming you know the basics of a sale.

**TIP**

One compromise that many successful "By Owner" sellers make is to set a time limit for selling. They give themselves a month or three months or whatever. If they don't sell within that time frame, they then bite the bullet and list. This is an excellent plan because it keeps you from wasting time and from losing out on a sale. Maybe you can sell it yourself; maybe you can't. The time limit helps you answer this question.

## Should You Really Do It?

Try this decision sheet to help you make up your mind.

### Selling "By Owner" Decision Checklist

1. Do you know the condition of the housing market in your area? \_\_\_\_\_
2. Are you clear on the steps in selling a home? \_\_\_\_\_
3. Are you up to date on the disclosure requirements, needed documents, and real estate law in your area? \_\_\_\_\_

4. Are you okay with handling people who are
   looking through your home?                          _____

5. Are you agreeable to letting strangers enter
   your home?                                          _____

6. Will you give up your weekends and evenings
   to show your home to potential buyers?              _____

7. Do you have a plan for handling the sales
   agreement, and who will fill it out?                _____

8. Do you have a plan for handling disputes with
   the buyer, both before and after an offer
   is presented?                                       _____

9. Have you worked out the financing so that you
   can give the buyer options?                         _____

10. Have you contacted an escrow company, a real
    estate attorney, and an agent, and has each
    agreed to handle a specific part of the deal?      _____

11. Have you readied an ad and are you willing to
    stick a "For Sale By Owner" sign in your
    front yard?                                        _____

# The Lease Option Option

Can't sell because the market's so bad?

But you have to move for a new job. Or you simply can't afford to sit there and make the payments. Or . . . ?

What do you do when you can't sell and have to move?

One option is the lease option. Here you can hang onto your existing home and rent it, typically for more than market rent. And, as part of the deal, you get a buyer who may just purchase it in a few years.

## What Is a Lease Option?

A lease option is a combination of a rental lease on your home plus an option to buy all rolled into one neat package. (There are ready-made lease option forms available in stationery stores. However, I suggest that if you purchase one, you do *not* use it as is and instead get an attorney to modify it to your specific needs—see the next TRAP.)

A lease option is for a set period of time (usually for one year or longer), a set amount of money payable monthly, and typical rental conditions. In addition, at the *tenant's* option, he or she can *purchase* the property up to a certain date (usually two or three years in the future), typically for a price agreed upon now. Sometimes cash must be put up to pay for the option privilege, although in a lease option, the lease itself is often considered enough.

Typically under a lease option, the tenant pays more than market rent each month, a portion of which is applied toward a future down payment should the tenant exercise the option portion and buy the property.

The lease option has many attractive elements for both the seller of a home and a potential buyer.

**TRAP**

Several states, such as Texas, have begun restricting the lease option. Usually they are concerned that the seller/landlord actually owns a realistic equity in the house and can eventually convey title. Check with a good attorney or agent in your state to learn about any restrictions on the lease option that could apply to you.

## Why Would the Buyer Want a Lease Option?

Buyers are typically short on cash. They don't have the funds necessary to make the down payment. With a lease option, however, they can tie up a house, move in, and accumulate at least part of the down payment right along with their rent. (Remember, a portion of the rent typically goes toward the down.) Let's take an example.

### Lease Option Example

Peter and Sally want to buy your home and are agreeable to paying the $200,000 you're asking. But they don't have the necessary 10 percent down payment ($20,000). So you offer them a lease option. You'll rent it to them for $1,500 a month (the lease). Of that $1,500, $1,000 will actually be rent and $500 will go toward a future down payment. When they have accumulated enough money for the down payment (about four years), you will credit them with the money and they will exercise their option and buy your property.

It's a neat scheme and many times it goes off without a hitch. The tenants pay the rent, accumulate the down, and are able to buy the property. It takes the buyers a little longer, but they do live in the property and, eventually, end up owning it.

## Why Would You Want to Give a Lease Option?

1. You have the chance for a sale in a market where sales may be hard to find. There are a lot more people out there who can pay a higher rent than can come up with a cash down. Find one of those, agree to a lease option, and look forward to selling your house, albeit a few years down the road.

2. You immediately remove the problem of making payments on your own toward your current mortgage, taxes, and insurance. By renting out the property you get immediate income. And because the rental is for more than the rental market rate (the money that is accumulating toward the down payment), you usually come close enough to make ends meet. If you've moved out of your home and are worrying about making the mortgage payments, this can be a wonderful solution.

3. You don't have to worry about maintaining the property. Remember, your tenants are the future owners. They have a vested interest in keeping it in great shape. Further, many lease option agreements provide that the tenants will pay for all minor repairs themselves.

**TIP**

You not only get a good tenant, but also a tenant who pays for repairs! It's a landlord's dream come true.

4. The tenants may not choose to exercise the option. After several years, for reasons we shall explore in a moment, they may decide not to buy. In that case, you—the seller—get the property back, frequently in excellent shape, and can keep all the extra money the tenants were paying in rent!

Is it any wonder that many sellers look eagerly toward a lease option as a wonderful out in a tight market?

## Are There Any Problems with the Lease Option?

Be aware that the lease option is not a panacea.

A good rule to follow in real estate as well as in life is that if something appears to be too good to be true, it usually is. That's frequently the case with a lease option.

Typically, when you first enter into a lease option, things are wonderful. The tenants pay on time and are quite content.

However, as time goes by, the tenants may begin to see the additional rent as a burden. It may be difficult for them to make the hefty monthly payments.

Further, unless the tenants have excellent credit, they may begin to realize that even if they accumulate enough for a down payment, they may not be able to qualify for a new mortgage, meaning they won't be able to exercise their option—which in turn  means they'll lose all the extra rent money they are paying.

Once the tenants realize that there is no light at the end of the tunnel and that the purchase of your home isn't realistic, they may bail out. They may simply walk away. In so doing, they could leave your property a mess.

**TRAP**

My own experience with lease options has been a mixed bag. In the worst case, I've had tenants, whom I found, that qualified for financing, but got into financial trouble, deserted the home, and left it a wreck. Don't think it can't happen to you.

No matter how careful you are, a tenant bailing on a lease option is always a real possibility. Here is a list of some of the things that can go wrong with a lease option.

### Things That Can Go Wrong

1. Tenants can't make the rental payment.
2. Tenants discover, after living in the property, that they don't like it and don't want to buy it.
3. Tenants aren't qualified to get a new mortgage and can't make the purchase.
4. Mortgage rates rise and previously qualified tenants now can't get a loan.
5. Tenants stop making payments and move out, leaving property a mess.

You can do some things that will help ensure a better ending to your lease option.

## How to Help Protect Yourself in a Lease Option

### Qualify Your Tenant/Buyers

Before going through with a lease option, have your tenant/buyers visit a mortgage broker or bank and get a letter stating that they currently qualify for a mortgage big enough to make the sale. That doesn't guarantee they'll qualify later on when they try to exercise the option (rates could change, as could their financial situation), but it at least shows they have the potential of qualifying.

### Make the Rent High Enough So Tenants Can Realistically Accumulate the Down

This an important point. Say your house is selling for $400,000 and the tenant/buyers need $40,000. If the amount accumulating from extra rent is only $100 a month and the lease option runs for three years, they will have accumulated only $3,600 by the time they need to exercise the option—not nearly enough. (And they probably won't have saved the balance on the side by themselves, either.) On the other hand, if $1,000 a month goes toward the option, at the end of three years they'll have a $36,000 credit—almost there.

Setting too low an amount of the rent for the future down payment is a recipe for failure with a lease option.

## Be Receptive to Reasonable Complaints About the Property

While the tenant/buyers can be expected to handle minor problems, major ones need cooperative efforts. They can handle a leaky faucet, but what about a new roof that's needed and costs $10,000? You'll have to work out a compromise and pay part or most of it yourself. If you insist that they pay for unreasonable expenses, they'll walk.

## Set a Price Now

It's not necessary to fix a price. You can agree that the price will be what an appraiser (or the average of three real estate agents) says it will be at a future date. But that tends to make would-be tenant/buyers nervous. It should do the same for you if prices have been falling in your area.

It's important that you and the would-be buyers know what the goal is. Maybe it's a $150,000 price or $300,000 or $75,000. Both you and the tenant/buyers need to know.

**TIP**

It is possible to include an inflation clause or market appreciation clause in a price. The price, for example, is $200,000, plus the cost of inflation annually, or the increase (or decrease?) in housing prices annually, or whatever. Be aware, however: the prospective tenant/buyers are not likely to look favorably on such a clause.

## If You Have the Property Listed, Do You Still Owe a Commission?

Often people who do lease options already have their property listed. How do you get the agent to withdraw the listing?

You could always wait until it expires. But usually the agent is willing to handle the lease option for you. Indeed, the agent may bring it to you.

Typically the agent receives a fee for the option. It's less than a sales commission, but is usually substantial, perhaps one or two months' rent. Further, if the buyers later exercise their option, then the agent gets the full commission. (That's why agents like this—it's better than having the listing expire without a sale!)

## Should You Try It?

For most of us, the lease option is another alternative. It can get you out of a financial hole, quickly. But just remember that it's not without its problems and it's not a cure-all.

# Finding Buyers by Offering Creative Financing

For every buyer who can pay you cash—who has a down payment and can get financing—there's another who either doesn't have the requisite down payment or who can't qualify for the mortgage. That buyer often goes by the wayside and doesn't get considered. However, when the market's tight, why overlook any buyers? Why not consider everyone who wants to buy your home, even if you have to handle all or part of the financing yourself? Why not consider what otherwise might be "throwaway" buyers?

## Why Finance It Yourself?

1. **You can make a deal that otherwise couldn't be made.**
   Maybe the buyer can't qualify for a large or low down payment institutional loan, but, it's the only buyer to come in

a long time. You have a large equity in the property, so you give the buyer a loan and make the deal.

2. **You want the higher interest.** Often people who are retired and have large equities in their homes are looking to sell and then put their money to work earning interest for them. But when interest rates at banks are very low, that's hard to accomplish. So they give the seller a mortgage and get an interest rate on it that's two to three times higher than the bank may offer.

3. **You can get a higher price.** Sometimes buyers are willing to pay more for a property if the seller will finance it. The reason, of course, is that the seller doesn't charge points or other large fees that other lenders charge. Thus, the buyer is willing to compensate by paying a higher price.

## What Is Seller Financing?

When you go into the grocery store and buy a jar of mayonnaise, normally you would pay all cash. You'd give the clerk your $3 or $4 or whatever for the mayonnaise. That would be the end of the transaction.

Selling real estate is rarely that simple, particularly in today's high priced market. Few, very few, buyers have cash to pay for the purchase of your home. Rather, they plan to finance most of the purchase price, typically up to 90 percent or more of it.

The usual route for financing is to go to an institutional lender: a bank, a savings and loan, or a mortgage banker. This lender gives the buyer the money usually in exchange for a trust deed—a variation of a mortgage, but more commonly used—on the property.

The buyer now gives you the combined money (the down payment and the proceeds of the mortgage) and the deal is made.

However, as noted, sometimes the buyers don't have the down or can't get financing from the institutional lender. Instead, they come to you and say, "Seller, please finance my purchase of your home." They may want you to carry back a second or third mortgage for all or a portion of the purchase price. If you own your home free and clear, they may even want you to carry back a first mortgage for the full amount.

TIP

Seller, or "creative," financing is when you receive "paper" (mortgage or trust deed) instead of cash for your sale.

Of course, the real question for you, the seller, is: Should I do it? Should I finance my property for the buyer?

Whenever someone wants me to do something, I'm usually wary. Why would the buyer want me to carry back a mortgage?

## Reasons Buyers Want You to Carry the Financing

1. The buyers have bad credit and/or don't have sufficient income and can't get an institutional loan.
2. The buyers don't have enough cash for the down payment.
3. Interest rates are so high that the buyers can't qualify for a mortgage.
4. The buyers are investors and they are looking to get a better deal by having you carry the financing.

### Seller Financing Example #1

Marcus has a house in Las Vegas. This was a booming area from 2002 to 2006, and builders put up thousands of homes. When the market took a nosedive, a lot of those sellers were forced or wanted to move out.

The market became extremely competitive. Marcus has been trying to sell his home for some time, without luck.

So Marcus told his agent that he was willing to carry 10 percent of the price in the form of paper. A buyer only had to pay 5 percent down (plus closing costs) to move in, getting an 85 percent mortgage.

The agent acknowledged that would help and soon found a buyer who purchased for 5 percent, with Marcus carrying paper.

Marcus's "paper" was in the form of a second mortgage for 10 percent down. The first mortgage was an 85 percent mortgage for the balance from a lender. He would receive payments of $200 a month for three years. After that time the buyer would owe a balloon payment of $20,000.

The deal closed, Marcus moved, and the buyer moved in. It's been nearly a year and Marcus has received the monthly $200 like clock-work. Of course, he worries in the back of his mind that maybe the buyer won't be able to refinance at the end of three years and pay off the balloon.

## Seller Financing Example #2

Ann also lived in Las Vegas and had the same trouble with selling as Marcus. However, she was desperate to get out. After months of no buyers, her agent suggested she handle the financing. She jumped at the chance. Ann agreed to carry 20 percent of the purchase price, with the buyer coming up with an 80 percent mortgage. She even agreed to pay for most of the buyer's closing costs. The buyer only needed $2,000—nothing down—to buy the property and move in.

The agent found a buyer within a week and Ann was thrilled. The deal closed a month later and she was out. According to the terms of the second mortgage she signed, the buyer would also pay her $200 a month for three years until a balloon of $30,000 came due.

Things went well for a few months then she stopped getting her $200 monthly payment. She called the buyers and they said they had both lost their jobs. They would pay her as soon as they found new work.

Ann waited three months. When she called back she discovered that the phone was disconnected. She flew to Las Vegas (having since moved to Los Angeles) and was shocked to discover her home was vacant. The new buyers had simply packed up and left. Worse, van-dals had broken in and severely damaged it to the tune of around $15,000.

Ann called the agent who had handled the sale and asked him what she should do. He gave her two rather bleak options:

1. She could begin foreclosure proceedings and take back the property. However, to do so she would have to make up the back payments on the first mortgage, which was several thousand dollars at that point, since the buyers hadn't been paying on the first, either. She also had to pay back taxes and foreclosure costs, which amounted to another few thousand or so. Once she got the house back in her name, she would need to refurbish it to the tune of another $15,000.
2. Or, she could simply walk away from the property as the buyers had done and lose all of her second mortgage.

Ann didn't have the money to take back the property and fix it up. So she walked away from her second mortgage, while the first foreclosed. She lost her equity in the term of the second mortgage.

## Cash Rules

Two stories, two different outcomes.

The reason that Marcus had at least an initial success was the down payment. Even as little as 5 percent down plus closing costs meant the buyers had a vested interest in the property, in keeping it up, and making payments.

With almost nothing put into Ann's property, the buyers had less invested than tenants. When things didn't go well for them, it was easy to move out.

The moral here is that if you're going to carry paper, be sure the buyers put up some cash in the form of a down payment and closing costs. The 5 percent in our example is the minimum—it's much safer for you if they put up 10 percent or more.

**TRAP**

Seller financing is inherently risky. However, you may be willing to accept the risk to get out of the property.

Top-notch buyers who have credit and cash don't need seller financing. They have cash for a down payment to keep their payments low and they don't have problems qualifying for a mortgage.

On the other hand, buyers who don't have cash or who can't get new financing are looking for seller financing. Thus, sellers who carry back paper are sometimes getting less able buyers, people who can't (or won't) keep up the payments if times get rough. These may be people who already have such bad credit that they don't mind walking away.

## Be Wary of Speculators

There's another category of buyers: speculators. Many speculators are "flippers," those who buy with an eye toward making a profit by quickly reselling (flipping) your home.

These people often buy property with seller financing, then try to resell. If they can, you can be paid off. If they can't, they may walk and you're stuck.

### Seller Financing Example #3

Chuck was about to retire. He had social security, but wasn't sure that it would be enough to live on during retirement. He wanted another source of income. His biggest asset was the equity in his home, which was paid off. Chuck's goal was to sell his home, put the money he received in the bank, and live off the interest.

However, at the time, the bank's highest interest rate was around 2 percent. Since Chuck had about $250,000 that he would get from the sale of the home, that meant he would receive roughly $5,000 a year. He needed a lot more.

When it came time to sell, the agent suggested that instead of looking for a buyer who would get a new institutional loan, Chuck should carry the first mortgage. Firsts were then paying about 6 percent interest, which would translate to about $15,000 a year in income for him.

In addition, if he made the loan for 20 years, he could be fairly assured of a steady income for a long time to come.

Chuck thought it was a good idea.

When buyers were found, the agent qualified them just as though they were getting a new institutional loan. They had to have a good credit score and they had to have sufficient income to "qualify"— roughly three times the monthly payment after all long-term debt, such as car payments. They also had to have a down payment of at least 10 percent.

The buyers purchased and Chuck carried back the financing. It's been several years now and Chuck's monthly check hasn't been late once.

A large part of the reason behind Chuck's success (and Ann's failure) has to do with their motivation in carrying back paper. In Ann's case, she felt it was the only way to make a sale and get out. Consequently, she was willing to accept less than desirable buyers (or at least not properly qualify them) and unfavorable terms.

In Chuck's case, however, the motivation was long-term income. Chuck was willing to sell only under favorable terms and to buyers who were qualified.

**TIP**

Be aware of your motives when you carry back paper. If you're desperate to sell and use seller financing to attract a buyer, be aware that you might get a less than desirable buyer. You might end up losing more than you gain by making the sale.

## The Sellers Who Outsmart the Bad Buyers

Some savvy sellers actually go looking for seller financing in the hopes of increasing their profits on the sale by taking advantage of an unwary buyer.

Here, the sellers' goal is to sell their property to a buyer in the hopes that the buyer will, in fact, default after a year or so. Then the sellers can get the property back through foreclosure. In this way, they can keep reselling the same property over and over!

There are two catches here. First, the sellers have to keep their costs down. These sellers typically sell FSBO, on their own, so they don't have any commission to pay. Their only expenses are the closing costs when they sell, the foreclosure costs later on if they have to take the property back, and any refurbishing they need to do.

Second, they get a large enough down payment from the buyers to cover all their costs plus a profit. Thus, when they take the property back, they're still in the black. And then they sell it again.

I'm not advocating this approach. I'm simply mentioning it to point out that if you want to play the game as a seller, you can play it to win.

## The Sellers Who Convert Paper into Cash

Paper taken back by a seller can be converted to cash, depending on a number of variables. Here's how sellers can take advantage of this conversion.

The sellers have a house to sell, which they feel is worth $200,000 on the market in a cash deal. They put it up for sale at $210,000 and offer to take partial paper.

Buyers, presumably, are willing to pay a little more for the house, since they don't have to put up all the cash up front. The deal is made. The buyers move and begin making payments to the sellers on a second mortgage.

The sellers wait at least six months, during which time the buyers (hopefully) make regular monthly payments on the second mortgage. Then the sellers sell that second mortgage to an investor in paper for cash. The sellers end up with a cash profit.

The advantage of this sale is that, with luck, the sellers are able to move the house faster by offering to carry back some of the paper than by waiting for all-cash buyers to make some extra money.

## Why the Six-Month Wait?

I'm sure some readers are wondering why the sellers waited six months before converting the second to cash.

Indeed, the sellers could have converted that note to cash in escrow. (This is sometimes done.) However, buyers of second notes—investors who are looking to make a higher interest on their cash—are wary of "unseasoned" seconds. They don't know if the buyer will actually make the payments or will simply default. Buyers of seconds don't normally want to get involved in foreclosure.

If you sell a second mortgage in escrow, the buyer of that second will normally pay less than if you let it "age" for a minimum of six months. Our sellers waited six months to be sure that they got top dollar (around 70 percent of the face value) for selling the second.

## Why Only 70 Percent of Face Value?

A second question many readers are sure to ask is why didn't the buyers of the second pay the full face value of the second in cash? Why was there a 30 percent discount?

The reason has to do with yield and risk. Yield is the actual percentage rate of interest that a buyer of mortgages gets. It is computed in a fairly complex formula that takes into account the interest rate, the amount of cash paid out, and the term.

## Yield Example

A second mortgage for three years may have a stated interest rate of 12 percent. However, because of the risk of foreclosure in the second mortgage market, an investor may demand a yield of 18 percent. How does he or she get that yield from a 12 percent mortgage? The answer is by discounting the second mortgage. A 12 percent mortgage which pays $15,000 at maturity, but which costs the buyer of that mortgage only $10,000 in cash, will in fact yield upward of 18 percent interest. (The 18 percent is figured on the $10,000 actually invested.)

Thus, by discounting the second mortgage, the seller is able to find an investor who is willing to buy it for cash.

**TIP**

The trick with offers to carry back a second with the intention of converting it to cash is this: get a high enough second. You need to have enough leeway so that when you sell at discount, you still get out the cash you want.

## What Makes a Second Mortgage Salable?

Finally, it's important to understand that simply taking back a second mortgage as part of seller financing doesn't guarantee you can resell it. Here's what investors are looking for in seconds:

### What Second Mortgage Buyers Look For

1. **High interest rate.** The higher the better.
2. **A short term.** Longer terms mean that the investor's money is tied up against an uncertain future when interest rate fluctuations could reduce the value of the second.
3. **A late payment penalty.** This is important. The second should contain a money penalty if the buyers are more than a couple of weeks late in their payment. The reason is simple. If there is no penalty, then each time the buyers are late, the holder of the second has only one option: start foreclosure, an expensive proposition. On the other hand, if the second has a penalty, it is easy to enforce and encourages prompt payment.
4. **Proper documents.** Improper documents or documents that are improperly executed account for more failures of

seconds than people realize. If you're giving a second as part of the sale, be sure you have a competent attorney check out the documents to be sure that they are properly drawn and executed.

## What About Balloon Payments?

Finally, there is the matter of balloon payments and second mortgages. Often second mortgages will have a final payment that is much higher than all the other payments, called a "balloon." This is the case when the interest rate is too low to allow the payoff of the mortgage or the term is too short.

If all goes well, this will work out fine for the seller. At the end of the term of the mortgage—say, four years—the buyers will refinance and fully pay off the seller. You get your monthly payments *and* your final payoff!

Sometimes, however, it doesn't go smoothly.

The buyers at the end of the short term of the second mortgage normally have to refinance to get enough cash to pay off the balloon. However, if the buyers can't refinance, then they can't pay it off. And if they then can't resell, as has happened in recent years, the seller is left holding the bag.

For this reason, many sellers at the end of the second mortgage term will offer to extend the mortgage for an additional term of years at what is the current interest rate. In this way, the seller preserves capital while receiving a good interest rate on it.

## Checklist for Seller Financing

1. Are you getting the current market interest rate for seconds? (It's much higher than for first mortgages.)
   *Check with agents, with the local paper under ads for seconds for sale, and with mortgage brokers to find the current rate.*

2. Are you giving the right term?

   *Seconds over five years are sometimes considered too long-term to be salable.*

3. Have you checked out the buyers' credit?

   *You can get a credit report either directly from a credit agency or through your agent. If the buyers have any bad credit at all, you're significantly increasing your risk of having to take the property back.*

4. Have you gotten an estimate of foreclosure costs in your area?

   *There are professionals who specialize in handling foreclosures. They often advertise under real estate in the classified section of papers. Or you can contact an escrow officer or a real estate agent who can direct you to one. Find out your likely costs now, before you commit.*

5. Are the buyers putting enough of their cash into the property?

   *The more cash the buyers put in, the more committed they will be to holding onto the property and avoiding default. Beware of buyers who put no cash down.*

6. Are you careful to *avoid* having a subordination clause in your second?

   *A subordination clause makes your second "subordinate" to another mortgage. What this means is that the buyers could refinance the first for more money, making your second worth less. Usually avoid this like the plague.*

7. Are your documents correct?

   *The only way to have any sense of security here is to have your documents examined by (if not prepared by) a competent real estate attorney.*

8. Have you consulted an attorney and a tax planner/ accountant to inform you of the tax consequences of getting a second mortgage?

*In some cases, even though you got back paper, the government may treat the sale as a cash sale and could require you to pay tax on the money that you didn't yet receive!*

9. Have you consulted with an expert on seller financing in your area to see if you're handling the deal correctly?

*Each state has somewhat different laws and rules regarding second mortgages. Be sure you're in compliance in your state.*

# Extreme Selling

In a challenging market when traditional home sales tactics aren't working, sometimes it's necessary to go to the extreme to get buyers interested in your house. Too many sellers and too many houses mean that buyers are overwhelmed with choices. You have to do something to make your home stand out.

Of course, you could simply lower your price until your house became such a bargain that buyers simply couldn't turn away. A neighbor of mine did that by lowering her price $15,000 every two weeks. Her home was sold six weeks later.

Of course, you're probably looking for a less dramatic way to get a sale than to cut the price out from under your property. That's what we'll consider in this chapter.

## Range Pricing

This is a technique that came into vogue during the housing bubble, when prices were escalating upward and multiple offers were the rule. Rather than ask for a single price, the seller (with the aid of his or her agent), would ask for a range of prices.

For example, instead of pricing the home at market at $400,000, the seller would "entertain" offers starting at $400,000 and upward to $500,000. Since there was a shortage of homes for sale at the time, very often within days the seller would receive offers closer to $500,000 and sometimes even higher! The result was that the home would eventually sell for above the perceived market value.

I've seen this same technique applied in a down market, also with good results, where the seller was happy to sell the property for close to or slightly below market value. (Remember, it was a down market when nothing was selling.)

Here the homeowner (again with the aid of a precocious agent) put the house up for sale at a range of prices. At the time the perceived market price for the home was about $350,000. The property was advertised (in the newspaper and with flyers) in the following manner:

### Advertisement for Range Pricing

SEALED BID SALE
The seller will entertain sealed bid offers
from $325,000 to $375,000 on Tuesday, October 7.

Of course, the agent's name, phone number, and address were given, as was the property address and description. On the first try, no offers came in until the Tuesday sale, and then almost half a dozen were received.

The first time I saw someone try this, all the offers were rejected by the seller. The lowest was for $210,000 (regardless of what the advertisement said) and the highest was for $320,000. The latter, of course, wasn't bad and was almost within the parameters of the sale. But, the seller wanted more. So the whole thing was tried again two weeks later, when the high offer was

$347,000, which the seller jumped at. (After all, it was close to the perceived market value.)

There was also a backup offer at $330,000.

The whole idea here is to avoid having a certain fixed price for the home that might cause buyers to ignore it. Remember, in a declining market, it's difficult to determine the actual market value of any property. When prices are falling, all the comps tend to be higher than what houses actually sell for. Range pricing lets the buyers determine the price—which, of course, they do anyway. Furthermore, having a price *range* suggests to buyers that perhaps a bargain is available.

Additionally, the sealed bid aspect and having the bids opened on a particular day adds the allure of an auction.

**TRAP**

Be careful of advertising a home for sale with a sealed bid without first checking with an attorney conversant with auctions in your state. Some states may define this as an auction and require that it be conducted by a licensed auctioneer. They may also have strict rules regarding deposits, paperwork, and whether the auction can be "absolute" (lowest bid wins no matter what) or "reserved" (the seller establishes a minimum bid—the reserve—below which he or she won't sell).

In one example I observed, the agent did not advertise an auction. Rather, the agent simply said that the house was range priced and that on a certain day the seller would "entertain" sealed bids. It was no more than what agents do all the time when they ask for offers, except that a day was stated and a range given.

It was inspired marketing. And in a down market, it very quickly netted a sale at a relatively good price.

## Contests

A homeowner in Oregon tried this, as have other homeowners in different states at different times. Essentially, it's an essay contest.

Write a hundred words telling the seller why you want to own the house. The entry fee was a couple of hundred dollars. Paying the fee and submitting the essay entered you in the contest.

The seller's goal, of course, was to sell several thousand entries, enough to pay for the house. When that was accomplished, the seller would gladly pick an essay winner and give the house away.

A neat trick. Can you do it?

A lot depends on how well you can promote the contest. Get the information out to enough people and you'll be able to sell all the entries you need. If you don't let people know or don't have an appealing enough campaign, you won't get entries.

On the other hand, getting thousands of people to part with a couple of hundred dollars apiece is no easy task. And what do you do if by the end of the contest you've only sold half the requisite number of entries? Do you refund the money? Do you give the house away anyhow?

**TRAP**

There are rules governing contests, state by state and federally. For example, if you require an entry fee (as opposed to, say, a "donation"), your contest may be deemed a lottery, which is governed by strict gambling laws. Be sure to check with an attorney conversant with running a contest in your state before attempting it.

Contests are an extreme way of trying to dispose of a house. I doubt a hundred people have successfully done it nationwide. However, if you have the time, the energy, and the daring, it might be something to consider.

## Auctions

Auction houses that specialize in real estate are springing up across the country. (Google "real estate auctions" to find one in your area.) They offer to sell your house to the highest bidder at auction. Of course, they will want a healthy commission for their work.

These auction houses primarily work with two groups of sellers. These are new-home builders who find themselves stuck with a lot of unsold yet built-out homes, and lenders who want to dispose of their REOs. (An REO is real estate owned by the lender taken in through foreclosure.)

Some of the auctioneers, however, will occasionally accept homes from individual sellers. They may even put together an auction strictly of individual homes. However, since this is a relatively new phenomenon and still catching on, you need to check with a home auctioneer in your area to see if they are handling sales of individual houses.

In a formal auction, you agree to sell your home to the highest bidder. There is usually a professional auctioneer, sometimes a tent is set up, and there may be champagne and refreshments. Almost always, there is a charged atmosphere of anticipation. Buyers come to auctions hoping to get a bargain. Sellers come to auctions hoping to sell their home quickly and for a good price.

The big thing to watch out for as a seller at an auction is the "reserve." This is the price below which you agree you won't sell your property. Set the reserve too high, and you won't get any acceptable bids. Set it too low, and you could end up giving your home away.

**TIP**

As noted earlier, there are also "absolute" auctions where there is no reserve. Beware of these. If someone bids $1 and it's the only bid, you'd be compelled to sell your home for that price!

For the seller, keep in mind that you'll need to pay a fee or commission to the auctioneer. It might be 5 or 6 percent. Or it could be 10 percent or higher. It's usually negotiable.

Auctions tend to work best with custom homes, those that are different from all the others nearby. If your home has unusual qualities, or is hard to price because of its design, location, or appearance, you may want to consider an auction. It could do well.

Keep in mind, however, that auctions take time to set up and hold. There can be a preparation period of a month or more while the auction house (through flyers, e-mails, advertising, and so on) builds interest in the sale. Unless you strike a deal in which you are allowed to continue selling your home on your own, that's time off the market for your property. And, if your home doesn't sell, it's back to square one after the auction.

**TRAP**

You might think about holding your own single-house auction. If so, as noted with range pricing above, first check with an attorney conversant with auctions in your state. Your state may have strict rules regarding how an auction is to be conducted.

Also, before signing up with an auction house, do your due diligence. You must make sure they are licensed, have a good rating with the Better Business Bureau, have no complaints against them with the district attorney's office, and can provide you with a list of satisfied customers you can call for reference.

## Incentives

These include almost anything you can think of, from flat screen TVs, to boats, to trips to Hawaii. And they are given not only to the buyers, but also to the real estate agents who bring in the buyers (which, as we'll see, may be more important).

The idea here is the same tried-and-true method that the "big guys," such as new home builders, use to move their product. Perhaps the best examples are when you tour a timeshare development. The incentives just to get you there may include free or reduced stays at a resort, gift certificates at local stores worth hundreds of dollars, and free meals at local restaurants. Once at the presentation, incentives may include points in travel or hotel clubs, reduced prices, and special vacation deals.

I suppose that many people are motivated to make a purchase on the basis of these incentives. Sellers that use them often rave about the results.

However, from my experience, the biggest motivator is still cash. Want to get a buyer to act? Take $5,000 or $10,000 off the price.

It's different, however, when you list with a real estate agent. When you list your property, if you put it on the MLS, you're tying into the network that links almost all the agents in your area. And probably 90 percent of homes are sold through those agents.

However, just because you're in the link doesn't mean that most, or even many, of those agents will pay any attention to your home. In a challenging market, your house is just one of thousands for sale in the area.

To get those agents' attention (the same agents who are going out with buyers every day), you need to distinguish your listing. And one excellent way to do that is with incentives.

You want to get the attention of as many agents as possible. And you want to build excitement in their minds about your property.

So why not give a 50-inch TV away to the agent who brings in the buyer that purchases your home? Why not a car lease? Or, perhaps you've got a boat, older but in good shape that you've been dying to get rid of. Give it to that agent who brings you a buyer. Don't think the agent won't be thrilled.

If you think it won't matter, you're wrong. I've seen agents come running to an agent's open house (held to attract agents, as opposed to buyers, to see the property) just because the seller was offering beer and cold sandwiches. Think what they'll do for real incentives!

## Neighborhood Open Homes

Are you in a tract where it seems like every other house is for sale? That can easily happen in a challenging market.

Usually it's a killer in terms of knocking down the neighborhood. Buyers who come by and see a wall of "For Sale" signs begin to wonder what's wrong with the area. Even worse, they begin to think about how difficult it might be for them to resell in a sea of homes that are for sale. As a result, they turn away, sometimes without even bothering to tour your home. The more neighboring homes for sale, usually the harder it is for you to sell yours.

This, however, is a case where you need to turn lemons into lemonade. Why not get all those for-sale homes working together? All it takes is a little initiative.

Of one thing you can be sure: your neighbors are just as desperate to sell as you are. So talk to them. Suggest that everyone on your street get together and have a neighborhood open house. It's sort of like a block party, but instead of being for the neighbors, it's for the buyers.

Then, using the combined resources of all the neighbors, advertise the heck out of it. "See 15 Homes Open at Once!" "The Biggest OPEN HOUSE Party of the Decade!" "Tour the Best Homes of Alderwood Estates!" You can make up dozens of slogans to entice buyers to come and see.

Be assured: buyers pick up on this kind of thing. Sure, you'll get your share of lookers, but, among them may be buyers. So be sure that you or your agent or both are on hand to get names and, hopefully, sign up deals.

The only real problem here is that not all of your for-sale neighbors are going to be helpful. Some may simply not see the benefits and not want to participate. Others may have their homes priced so high that the open house party won't help them. And yet others may have their homes priced so low that they'll detract from the price you're asking.

Compromise is necessary for a neighborhood open house to work. Just be persistent and keep pointing out the advantages. Usually, most of your neighbors eventually will come around.

## The Bottom Line

In a difficult market, you have to go the extra mile to get the buyer and the sale. "Take it to the extreme" is a phrase that could get you sold, and fast.

# Converting to a Rental and Holding On for Better Times

You can't sell. You can't refinance. But you probably *can* rent out your home. (This is especially true since in many areas, rental rates have gone up as the resale market has declined.)

Converting your present home to a rental is one of the easiest ways to start getting income from your home. And it could allow you to hang onto it until the market gets better and you can sell.

## How It's Done

My friend Carlos, who owns a house in a suburb of Los Angeles, was recently transferred to Denver. He could have put his L.A. house up for sale. But the market at the time was falling and he would have taken a big loss if he sold. Also, he felt if he hung onto it for a few more years and the market turned around, there would be lots of money to be made. So what did Carlos do?

He didn't give up his new job opportunity, and he didn't lose his old house. Instead he rented his home out with the understanding that in a few years, when the market turned around, he would sell—hopefully for a profit. He became a landlord.

This is not to say that becoming a landlord is all rent checks and peace of mind. It can be hard work, particularly if you are forced to move some distance away, but it can be manageable. People do it all the time. I've done it many times myself. And it may be your best alternative to selling.

## But What If You Need the Money from a Sale to Buy Your Next House?

Usually you can get some of your money out, even if you rent your current home. You can get it out by refinancing.

For example, let's say that your house is worth $400,000 and you owe $200,000. Your expenses of selling might run $30,000 (including commission), so you stand to net $170,000, if you could sell. You plan to use that $170,000 toward the purchase of your next house.

But instead of selling, you refinance it. As an *owner/occupant* you are entitled to almost the same terms as a new buyer when you refinance. You might get as much as 80 percent of its current value in a new loan, perhaps more. (If you were an investor who owned a rental property, most lenders would loan you enough only to pay off your existing mortgage and closing costs—they wouldn't let you take any cash out. Being an owner/occupant offers more opportunities.)

If your home is worth $400,000 you should be able to refinance up to $320,000 (80 percent). Minus your existing mortgage of $200,000 and roughly $5,000 in financing expenses, you could clear about $115,000. That should help you get into a new house! (And the tenants will help make that mortgage payment.)

TIP

Whether or not you're able to get favorable refinancing depends to a large degree on whether or not you are an owner/occupant. That means that you should try to secure all your financing *before* you move from your property. Once you have the mortgage on your property and live in it for an appropriate amount of time, most lenders don't care whether you continue to occupy it or rent it out.

## How Much Can You Rent Your Home For?

That's very important. Hopefully, you can rent your existing home for as much as or at least close to your mortgage payment, taxes, and insurance. This is called a "real estate break-even." It's not a true break-even because it doesn't include maintenance, repairs, and management. But hopefully, those will offset a loss you can show on your property through depreciation. (Check with your accountant as the rules are tricky here).

Here's how you determine what you can rent your home for:

### Finding What Your Home Will Rent For

1. **Contact local agents and ask them.** If they know your neighborhood and handle rentals, they should be able to tell you off-the-cuff.
2. **Look for existing rentals in your neighborhood.** Ask the owners what their rental rate is. Your house, if it's similar, should rent for about the same.
3. **Check your local paper under "Houses for Rent—Unfurnished."** Look for homes with the same number of bedrooms and baths as yours, and in similar areas, and see what others are charging.

**4. Check with rental management firms in your area.** You will probably be surprised. Today, rental rates are often higher than we anticipate.

Be sure to make your calculations accurately. Here's a little chart that will help you determine how much your basic expenses are.

**Rental Income versus PITI**

| | | |
|---|---|---|
| Rental Income | | $_____ |
| Less: Mortgage(s) | _____ | |
| Taxes | _____ | |
| Insurance | _____ | |
| PITI total | | −_____ |
| Postive (or negative) cash flow | | $_____ |

If you have positive cash flow (or even if you have a little negative cash flow), you probably have a property that's well suited, financially speaking, to be a rental. If expenses are high, however, and you have a large negative cash flow, then you may want to reconsider renting.

**TIP**

Don't fall into the mistaken belief that you won't have any other costs beyond PITI. As noted earlier, there will always be maintenance and fix-up expenses. However, you may be able to write off the losses—see your accountant about this—and this will help.

**TRAP**

If it turns out that your PITI expenses are far higher than your rental income, don't say "damn the torpedoes, full speed ahead!" When expenses exceed rental income, you move into negative cash flow territory. That means that each month—just to pay the mortgage, taxes, and insurance—you have to take money out of your own pocket. While this may seem easy to do when looking at it theoretically, it's quite different when you're faced with actually spending the money each month. You may quickly come to call that property a "bottomless pit." In the trade they have a name for such houses. They are called "alligators." They just keep biting at you.

## Do You Have a Landlord's Temperament?

My friend Phil decided to do just what has been described thus far in this chapter. He decided to convert his existing home to a rental. It made sense, financially. Philly, unfortunately, just wasn't the sort who made a good landlord. He managed to rent the property, and the first week after the tenants moved in, they called him at 11 p.m. to say that the sink in the master bathroom was dripping and they couldn't sleep. Could he please come over and fix it?

Those who rent property on a regular basis would have sweet talked the tenants, expressing concern and suggesting they turn the water off underneath the sink. They would then assure them that a plumber (or the landlord) would be out there first thing in the morning.

Philly, however, had just fallen asleep when the phone rang. When he heard the problem, his response was to shout into the phone that they were disturbing his own sleep and that the tenants could damned well fix their own faucet.

At the end of the month, the tenants moved out and Phil had to rent the place all over again.

The next tenants were better. They waited until the second week to call, complaining that their furnace wouldn't go on and that it was the middle of winter and they were cold.

Philly tried to handle it better. He suggested that they build a fire in the fireplace and he'd send out a heating repair person the next day. He did, and it turned out that the heat exchanger on his furnace was broken. He needed a new furnace to the tune of $3,200.

He exploded. He didn't have the cash available. He told the tenants they'd have to wait until the following month when he got the money to fix the furnace.

They moved out the next day and sued him in small claims court for the half-month's rent they said they had coming. He tried to argue with the judge, but when the tenants pointed out that he refused to fix the furnace during the cold of winter, he lost.

Philly's problems were not actually financial. They were psychological. (He could have borrowed the money to fix the furnace.)

He never quite understood that owning a rental property is like caring for a delicate flower. It has to be watered and pampered in order for it to prosper. Philly didn't want the bother and the headache. He wanted the rental to take care of itself. Unfortunately, that's not the way rentals are.

If you're like Phil, emotionally speaking, then you shouldn't personally rent out your home regardless of whether it makes financial sense. (The exception is if you're willing to pay a property management firm to handle it for you—but expect to pay them anywhere from 11 to 14 percent of your monthly rental income.)

In the end you'll lose money and perhaps even ruin your health, because you'll be doing something for which you are unsuited. On the other hand, millions of Americans personally rent millions of homes out each year without much hassle and much bother. And they eventually receive significant profits for doing so. It all depends on your mental attitude.

## How to Successfully Handle a Rental

Wei, a young woman living alone, found herself in the familiar predicament of having to move to a new home, yet not able to resell her old home.

So Wei decided to try renting out her old house. She borrowed against it (as described above) and used the money as a down payment on another house. Then she was faced with the realities of being a landlord.

Since her old house was already in good shape, she didn't have to do any fix-up work. She placed an ad in the local newspaper. It was a short, three-line ad which read:

**Rental Ad**

For Rent Lovely Garden Home,
3 bed, 2 bath with fireplace, den,
large garage $1,850.

Wei included her phone number and soon began receiving calls. She screened the prospective tenants to weed out those who could not afford the house or who had families too large for the property. Then she showed it.

Eventually, she got several people who wanted to rent. Wei picked up some rental application forms from a local real estate agent she was friends with and had the applicants fill them out. Then she chose the most likely prospect for a tenant and got a credit report on the person.

The credit report was terrible—the applicant never seemed to pay bills. So she picked the next likely candidate and got a credit report. This prospect had okay credit, so she rented the property, collecting the first month's rent plus a sizable cleaning/security deposit.

There have been, of course, maintenance problems. But Wei either corrected them herself or called in local people to do the job. In over two years of renting, she has had the same tenants and hasn't had any major problems. The housing market in her area has declined, but shows signs of bottoming out and returning. She's looking forward to the time, perhaps in a few years, when she can resell the property for a nice profit.

All of which is to say that if you're willing to devote a little time and energy to your rental, as well as use a bit of common sense, it's not that hard to find and keep good tenants and to make a profit on rental property. If you can't (or don't want to) sell your present house when you move, converting to a rental makes excellent sense in many circumstances.

For more details on handling rentals, look into the many Web sites that offer advice, rental forms, and professional help including:

www.thelpa.com (The Landlord Protection Agency)
www.landlordandinvestor.com
www.landlordassociation.org

# Special Help for Selling Condos and Co-ops

I s it harder to sell a condo or a co-op, especially when the market is rough?

Condominiums, with certain exceptions, have been looked upon as somewhat less desirable than houses in the past. As a result, for a given amount of square footage, condos have generally sold for less than single-family homes.

That all changed with the housing bubble. Suddenly, with prices of single-family detached housing shooting up, buyers began looking at condos as a less expensive alternative. That caused the price of condos to quickly rise. Indeed, by 2005, many condos, on a per square foot basis, were selling for more than single-family detached housing!

With the real estate market crash, that trend has slowed, if not reversed. Nevertheless, in many areas today, condos are still considered as desirable, if not more so, than other types of housing.

Yet even though there may be strong demand for condos (and co-ops) in your area, there are certain intrinsic elements that can make them more difficult to resell. We'll discuss some of these in this chapter.

## Can You Put Up a Sign That Can Be Seen?

With a single-family home, one of the best (if not *the* best) methods of advertising is to put a "For Sale" sign in the front yard. Since the front yard of a condo is owned by everyone in the association, you normally can't do that. Most condominium bylaws, in fact, preclude you from putting a "For Sale" sign for your condo in any common area. Thus, letting people know that you have a condo for sale can be difficult. But not impossible.

First, use an agent. The agent can meet buyers at his or her office and then bring them by.

Second, see if you can fudge on the sign. Try putting a sign in the window of your unit or on the garage door. If you face the street, you might be able to get some exposure. In any event, you can probably get away with it until another owner complains, or a condo director notices and takes issue.

**TRAP**

Some associations (condos have homeowner associations, co-ops have boards of directors) prohibit you from putting a sign on the exterior walls, on doors, or in the window of your own unit. Such rules can be hard to enforce, but strict homeowner associations and boards may try.

## How Do You Arrange for Showing?

With a single-family home, showing simply means having the buyers come by and take a look. If you're not home, a lockbox on the house can allow agents access with buyers.

With a condo or co-op, you must often get permission to get through a gate or door. This means that unless you want to give everyone the code to the gate (or a pass to the door), you must arrange for showings. Thus, it will take more time to show a condo or co-op for you . . . or your agent.

Plan on spending lots of weekends trying to sell your unit. It could take more time and effort than for a single-family home.

## Do You Have Your CC&Rs and Bylaws Available?

Condos and co-ops are not simply less expensive and smaller single-family homes. They are actually a different type of lifestyle—a shared lifestyle.

It's important that each buyer who comes by understands this. The best way to make sure is to have available a set of bylaws and CC&Rs (deed Conditions, Covenants, and Restrictions). That way, buyers can take a look at and see what you're actually offering.

**TRAP**

At some point, every buyer will be made aware of the bylaws and CC&Rs, either by the agent or by the homeowners association (HOA) or board. Better that you educate them early on. It will help them make an informed purchase decision, and you will save yourself a lot of time and aggravation since they could try to back out of the deal if they find out something they don't like late in the process.

Some sellers will offer a short list of the rules of the association or board to help buyers identify the restrictions and the amenities that are offered.

## Will Your Co-op Board Approve?

A co-op is actually a stock corporation. The board runs it and your evidence of ownership is usually in the form of stock and a lease on your unit.

That means that in order to sell, you often have to get the approval of the board. When the board gives approval, it will take back your stock and issue new stock to the buyer and a new lease. Of course, the sale is handled in the usual manner and you normally get your equity out in the form of cash.

**TRAP**

A co-op board may not refuse approval of a sale to a new buyer for reasons of race, religion, gender, national origin, or any other protected category. However, they may refuse approval on financial grounds—that the new owner doesn't have the financial wherewithal to afford the property.

This control that the board exerts is, in fact, one of the factors that may make your co-op more valuable and desirable. Many buyers like being able to have some control over who their neighbors will be.

The reason that co-ops often look carefully at a buyer's financial means is that they want to be sure that the buyer can make payments on a blanket mortgage that may cover all of the units. If one unit owner fails to pay, then the others must make up the difference. Thus, the other members, through their board, have a vested interest in seeing that your buyer is financially sound.

By first talking to the board, or at least the general manager, you will be able to get a sense of what the board is looking for in a new buyer, and save yourself a lot of wasted time and effort in bringing in someone who's not fully qualified.

With condos, you can generally sell to whomever you please. However, the new owners will have to abide by the general bylaws and other rules governing the development.

## Will the Architectural Committee Allow Any Changes to the Unit Buyers May Want?

Condo owners are typically restricted in terms of any changes they can make to the property. For example, if your unit lacks an interior washer and dryer, and your buyers want to install one. (Or you suggest to buyers they may want to install one as part of an inducement to purchase.)

However, the architectural committee may not give approval. And if it doesn't, your buyers won't be able to put in an interior washroom. (Installing an interior washroom could impact on the plumbing and noise of other unit owners.)

Be sure to check out any issues involving architectural changes before you list your unit. That way you can be prepared to handle questions about such changes from agents and potential buyers.

## Can Buyers Find Your Unit?

Whether you're selling by owner or through an agent, you can't show a unit unless the buyers can find it. With a single-family house, it's just a matter of giving a street address. With a condo or co-op, on the other hand, there's also the matter of finding the unit within the development.

Don't assume that everyone is as good with directions are you are. I've spent more time than I'd like wandering around condo developments and co-op buildings, lost and unable to find the unit I was searching for. (And I have excellent directional instincts!)

The best solution is to create a map of the development and/or building and give it to everyone who's interested. You can also put it up on a Web site, e-mail it, and fax it.

## Can You Overcome Dark Corners?

And old trick when showing homes is to always turn on all the lights. The home appears brighter and more enticing to potential buyers.

This rule is of particular significance to many condo and co-op sellers. The reason is that if your unit is in a larger building, chances are it has some access to the outdoors, probably front and rear. But very likely there are solid walls on both the sides. This means that, unlike a house, there is only half the opportunity for light from outdoors to penetrate and illuminate the interior.

I can tell you from experience, when showing condos where the owners did not turn on all the lights, buyers almost universally complain about how dark the place is inside—this on a bright sunny day. For many buyers it's the difference between making an offer and looking elsewhere.

If your unit is particularly dark, you may want to even go out and purchase extra lamps. You can get very bright inexpensive floor lamps (for around $30 a pop) and set them up in every room. It can make all the difference.

## Are There Lawsuits?

In recent years, it's almost unusual for a condo or co-op *not* to be involved in lawsuits of one sort or another. Sometimes it's the owners suing the builder over defects. At other times, it's the board or HOA suing an owner for failure to pay fees. Or an owner suing the development over restrictions. Or owners suing owners over grievances. Or legal problems with outsiders.

All of these lawsuits present an obstacle to selling your unit. Buyers don't like them. And lenders don't either.

The reason is that, depending on who wins and who loses, all of the members of the development might be asked to pay a sometimes sizable judgment. Thus, if you have a lawsuit pending, it could scare away a buyer or make it difficult for that buyer to obtain necessary financing.

It's important that you get a handle on any lawsuits and prepare an explanation for them to the buyer. You must also understand how they might impact that buyer's decision to make a purchase. Most boards and associations will provide this information to you and your buyer, but they can charge a fee. (*Note:* They may not provide the details of the case, but should be able to provide the names of the parties and other general information of record.)

It's a good idea to consult with a member of the board or association to learn what's out there and to get some background on it. Thus, when your buyer is alarmed about a lawsuit the board has against the builder, you can explain that it's over leaking roofs and that the insurance will cover most of it—but the Board is trying to recover the deductible, if that happens to be the case.

## Do You Have Congenial Neighbors?

With a single-family house, the neighbors are usually some distance away, and even if they are loud and raucous, you can usually live with them. With many condos and co-ops, however, the neighbors are as close as a next-door apartment. Loud noises in particular can be a real problem.

It's a good idea to disclose to buyers any problem neighbors you have. And get your disclosure in writing. That way, the buyers can't go back to you after the sale and say that you never told them so.

Yes, this could scare some buyers away. On the other hand, it could make your deal stick.

## Do the Buyers Understand the Lifestyle?

Try to be there when buyers come by. By all means, show them your unit. But then, take them on a tour of the development.

If you have these facilities, show off the:

- Swimming pool and spa
- Tennis courts
- Golf putting range
- Clubhouse
- Exercise room
- Any other amenity

If possible, point out how close your unit is to these facilities.

Sometimes buyers may decide to make a purchase not because they fall in love with your unit, but because they like the extra features your development offers. Sometimes they'll buy in spite of your unit, just to get the amenities!

## Can You Help with the Financing?

If there is some difficulty in getting financing with your unit, offer to carry some of the paper yourself. (See Chapter 9 for how to do this.)

Buyers might have difficulty finding a lender if, as noted above, the development has lots of lawsuits. They might have great difficulty getting financing if more than 25 percent of the development is rented out. (Lenders often steer clear of condos and co-ops that have a higher rental to owner ratio than 1 in 4. They figure that there's too much turnover and too much chance that owners are renting because they can't sell. That's not a good spot to place a loan.)

Thus, be prepared to offer a second mortgage for perhaps 10 to 20 percent or more of the purchase price. Assuming you have enough equity to do this, you'd get your money out in the form of paper instead of cash. (Again, check into Chapter 9 for converting paper to cash.)

## Can You Help with the Marketing?

Finally, if the market is not particularly strong for condos and co-ops in your area, your agent may not be willing to spend enough resources on your unit to get a sale. You may find this isn't just a failing of a particular agent, but a general mindset of all agents in the area. Yes they'll take your listing. But they figure it won't sell quickly or easily, so they aren't willing to push it.

If this is the case, you may need to help with the advertising as well as the marketing. (Reread Chapter 7 for tips on what do.) To compensate, you may want to look for a fee-for-service broker or a discount broker.

# Successful Negotiating in Any Market

Y ou've finally gotten an offer!

You got the call from the agent. There's an offer on your home. The agent is going to bring it by in just a short while.

Hooray! You're finally on your way out of this house and on with your life. You can hardly wait. At last it's over. The long ordeal has ended.

Wrong!

If you're like most sellers, the most difficult part of selling your home has just begun. When that agent or buyer comes over and you take a look at that offer, be prepared to be unsatisfied. The chances are very rare that it's going to be everything you're hoping for. Even in a hot market, even if the offer is for full price, you may feel you need, want, and can get more.

If it's a cold market, you'd better be sitting down when that offer comes in. It's likely to be for a price much lower than you want to accept, with terms that could be onerous to you. In other words, the offer has every chance of being unacceptable.

Only now does the real process of selling your house begin. You have to negotiate with the buyers to get what you want and need.

## The Counteroffer

In real estate, real negotiations take the form of "counteroffers." The buyers tell you that they're interested in your property with an offer. How you tell them that their offer is unacceptable, but that you're willing to negotiate, is the counteroffer.

Counteroffers often fly back and forth between buyer and seller, sometimes stretching into the wee hours of the morning. I've heard many sellers complain that the negotiations were the hardest, the most painful part of the entire sales procedure. One even moaned that it was worse than getting a tooth filled without anesthetic!

Our goal in this chapter is to take the pain out of negotiating and to get the best deal for you.

Of course, you could be lucky. A buyer could simply fall in love with your property and offer full price and just what you want in terms. But, quite frankly, that's not the way it usually works. In the vast majority of deals, it's now time to slug it out.

## What Do You Want?

In any negotiations there are winners and there are losers. Often the losers don't even know they lost for days, months, or even years later. But the winners always know they won. The reason is simple: winners define winning before they start.

In your case, you must know what you want. And in the event you cannot get it, you must also create a tentative fallback position of the minimum you will accept.

**TRAP**

You never know what the buyers will offer. Consequently, it's a mistake to form a rigid fallback position by saying, "I'll not take a penny less, no matter what!" Maybe the buyers will offer you something you never thought of—less than you want, but in a creative scheme that you had never considered and that has all sorts of other possibilities. Be open and consider all offers.

Let's face up to it. The price you're asking for your home and the terms you're demanding are part realism and part hope. What you must now do is get more realistic. Let's say that houses like yours have been selling in the $150,000 to $165,000 range. So you put your house up for $165,000. That's hope. Now an offer's coming in.

You've got to understand that to be realistic, you might have to accept less.

**TIP**

You never know how things are going to go and what you will do until you're in the heat of battle. I've sat with sellers who were staunchly determined not to accept a penny less than their asking price. Then, as soon as a much lower offer was made, they fawned all over the buyer's broker in their eagerness to accept. Be prepared for the unexpected, even in your own reactions.

Assuming that the offer is going to be presented by an agent (usually both the buyer's agent and your agent—the seller's agent—are present), you should be aware of the subtle pressures that can be brought to bear on you. Remember, after all, that usually neither agent gets a penny unless you agree to the offer.

In most cases where I've seen an offer being presented, the buyer's agent begins with a statement something like this: "I'm sure you'll agree with me that this is an excellent offer, probably a better offer than you might expect to get at this time. When you've had a chance to look it over thoroughly, I'm sure you'll realize how generous the buyer has been." You could be asking $200,000 and the buyer could be offering $100,000. You could be asking all cash and the buyer could be demanding that you carry 100 percent financing. Still, when the deal is presented, it always seems to be a "good" offer, the "best" offer, the most "favorable and generous" offer, and so on.

I once knew a very good agent who, when faced with presenting an offer that was far off the mark, would always begin by asking the sellers, "Are you creative people?" Most of us are hard-pressed to answer that we're not creative. When the sellers replied "yes," the agent would continue. "I knew it. I knew you'd be willing to look at this offer with an open mind, because it's a creative offer." The different ways to present an offer are unlimited, but it all usually comes down to the same thing. The agent tries to get you into a good mood, a mood of openness, and then hits you with the troubles.

## There's a Right Way to Receive an Offer

Most sellers have no idea how to receive an offer—called a sales agreement, a purchase offer, or sometimes a deposit receipt. In most cases, they sit there dumbly while the agent puts a copy filled with clauses and tiny writing in front of them and then proceeds to read through it line by line, often obscuring some of the most salient points.

The correct way to receive an offer is to take charge and direct the proceedings. Once in charge, you can quickly determine the strong and weak points of the offer and then start making your decisions.

When the agent begins, "This is how I like to proceed . . . ," interject with the following or similar comment: "This is my house and

I want to proceed in the following manner." Then list what you want to know in the order of importance to you. Here's a handy list of information items prioritized in the order you may wish to receive them:

### Questions to Ask When Receiving an Offer

1. **Deposit.** How much and who has it? (Is it a serious offer, as evidenced by a sufficient deposit?)
2. **Price.** What exactly are the buyers offering?
3. **Down payment.** Cash, and if not, why not?
4. **Terms.** New first loan? Any seller financing?
5. **Occupancy.** How soon do I have to get out?
6. **Contingencies.** Is there anything that could weaken the deal?

As you go through the above questions, be sure you understand the answers given to you. When you don't understand something, ask for an explanation. If you still don't understand, don't be hesitant to ask to have it explained again and again. Only a fool is afraid to ask a question when his or her money is at stake.

**TIP** You may hear a price substantially lower than what you're asking. The tendency is to throw up your hands and say, "No, never!" That's a mistake. Even if the price is low, the terms may make up for it, or vice versa. You seldom want to turn down an offer cold. Always try to counter.

## How Do You Tell a Good Offer from a Bad One?

You probably have a good idea of what you want and if you're not getting it, you're going to figure it's a bad offer.

Usually, however, offers aren't great or terrible. They're somewhere in between, with good points and bad points. All of which means you're going to have to probe to see if it has some fine points in your favor not initially brought out. It's not usually an easy call to decide if the offer should be accepted or not.

The buyers may give you some things you want in exchange for demanding others that you don't want to give up. For example, the buyers may give you your price, but insist on onerous terms such as a long-term mortgage for you to carry back at a low interest rate.

You have to decide. Is it worth accepting such terms in order to get price?

Or the buyers may insist that you be out of the house within 30 days. But, you protest, the kids are in school. You need at least 90 days. The agent makes it quite clear that the buyers have to be in within 30 days because that's when they're moving into the area.

The agent says they won't compromise. (Everyone will compromise a little.) Do you want to sell enough to move twice—once to a rental and a second time to your next home?

These are just a few of the trade-offs you may encounter. To help you make a decision, try the following decision-making procedure.

## Seller's Decision Maker

| | Pros | Points | | Cons | Points |
|---|---|---|---|---|---|
| 1. | _____ | ____ | 1. | _____ | ____ |
| 2. | _____ | ____ | 2. | _____ | ____ |
| 3. | _____ | ____ | 3. | _____ | ____ |
| 4. | _____ | ____ | 4. | _____ | ____ |
| 5. | _____ | ____ | 5. | _____ | ____ |
| | Total | ____ | | Total | ____ |

List the pros and cons of the offer on this or a similar sheet. Of course, the assigning of points to issues is going to be arbitrary and you may feel that it's silly to do it. If so, then at least consider listing the pros and cons so you can see what the trade-offs are.

The use of points is just an attempt to quantify the issues so that you can see at a glance which are more important and whether the preponderance of points is for or against.

## How Do You Handle Contingency Clauses?

In an offer, a contingency clause (also sometimes called a "subject to" clause) is usually a bad phrase to hear if you're a seller. A contingency clause means just what it says—the offer is contingent on some act happening which is described in the clause.

A contingency clause is sometimes handwritten into the offer and is an additional condition to all the boilerplate that's already part of the document. (Some common contingency clauses, such as one on financing, are often part of the boilerplate—the buyer just checks a box to put them into effect.) Sometimes it's written on the back of the document and initialed by the buyers. Be very careful of contingency clauses.

**TRAP**

Contingency clauses are often misunderstood by sellers because they are sometimes written in—instead of being part of—the prepared form of the offer. Be sure you understand all the implications of a contingency clause before you accept or reject it. If necessary, hold off making a decision on the offer until you've had your lawyer look at it and explain it to you.

### Some Typical Contingencies

Contingent sale. The buyers will purchase contingent on selling (translation: as soon as they sell) their present home. This is a very weak offer, because it means the sale of your house depends on the sale of another house with another set of sellers and buyers.

Financing. The buyers will purchase contingent on their getting new financing. You want to see their preapproval letter to find out if they're qualified. A financing contingency is most common.

Timing. The purchase is contingent on the buyers being able to move into the house within a set period. Good or bad depending on your own plans.

Disclosures/Inspections. The buyers will only purchase if they approve your disclosures and their professional inspection. Typically they will ask for a set period for this, usually a couple of weeks.

Frivolous. The buyers will purchase contingent on Uncle Todd's cow delivering a new calf—a frivolous offer.

Contingency clauses are ways for the buyers (and sometimes the sellers) to get out of the deal. When buyers insist on a contingency clause it's like telling you, "Yes we'll buy, if." It's the *if* that's the killer.

Your goal is to get as few of the buyers' contingency clauses as possible into the agreement and to limit by time and performance those which are included. Let's look at that more closely.

## Limiting the Contingency Clauses

Smart buyers will put few contingency clauses into an agreement—foolish or nervous buyers put many. The more you have in an offer presented to you, the more you need to be wary.

How do you handle contingency clauses? My suggestion is that you examine each one carefully and ask yourself three questions:

### Questions to Ask Yourself About Contingencies

1. **Is the contingency reasonable?** Making the purchase contingent upon getting financing is reasonable. Making it subject to Uncle Todd coming down and looking at the house in the next month or two isn't.

2. **Does this contingency negate the value of the offer?** The buyers offer all cash, contingent upon their final approval of the property one day before closing. There's no deal here, since the buyers can refuse the property at their option at any time right up to closing.

3. **Can I live with the contingency or should I limit it?** You can limit the contingency by insisting that it be performed within a specified time, say, seven days. Or you can demand that it be completely removed. Just remember that when you remove a contingency, you're making a counteroffer, which the buyers may not accept.

**TIP**

Remember, the offer to purchase is just that—an offer. You're not compelled to accept. The offer has no binding effect on you until you sign.

**TRAP**

You can't both accept and counter an offer. Once you change the offer in any way, even something so simple as to put a time limit on a contingency, you have effectively declined the offer. What you write in is now a new counteroffer, which must be submitted to the buyers and which they are under *no obligation* to accept.

If for any reason you can't live with the contingency as it now stands (it's not reasonable or it negates the rest of the offer), then you feel you must take action. Just remember, however, that the action you take may be to reject an offer that may never again be presented. If the buyers don't like what you counter with, they are under no obligation to accept it. They can simply pick up their marbles and leave.

## How Do You Make a Counteroffer?

When an offer to purchase is presented to you, you really have only three choices:

### Your Choices When You Receive an Offer

- You can accept it exactly as it is.
- You can reject it.
- You can reject it and then counter with an offer of your own.

Remember, *you cannot accept it and make changes in it*. As soon as you make any changes at all to the offer presented by the buyers, it's a brand new offer. You may, for example, like the offer—only the buyers want you out by the twentieth, which is a Friday; so you change it to the twenty-first, which is a Saturday, to give yourself more time to move. You've created a counteroffer.

When you reject the buyers' offer, they have every right to simply walk away from the potential deal. They wanted the date to be Friday the twentieth so *they* would have time to move. They won't budge. Besides, in the interim they've found a house they like more than yours, so they're not interested anymore. You've lost the deal.

**TIP**

If you possibly can live with it, it's often a good idea to accept the offer as it is presented. This assumes, of course, that the price, terms, and contingencies are all within your parameters. In other words, if the deal is very close to what you want, you may be making a mistake by trying to get the last penny or the last favorable term. By going for everything you want with a counteroffer, you risk losing what otherwise may be a sure deal.

Don't be confused by the physical form of the counter. A counter is a separate new offer. Only this time, instead of the buyers making an offer to you, you are making an offer to them.

This is can be confusing, since many agents write the counteroffer right on the back of the original offer, adding language to the effect that "seller accepts offer with the following changes." Then the changes are listed. It all sounds like you've accepted something.

In truth, you've rejected the offer and are presenting a new offer to the buyer. However, psychologically, many agents feel that if the new offer comes back on the same document and it appears that there are only a few changes, the buyers might be more willing to accept it. This is probably good psychology, although it makes for messy offers, particularly if the buyers then recounter your offer.

The important thing to remember is that each time you counter and each time the buyers counter, it's a new offer, regardless of how similar to the old offers it may be. You may end up only $100 apart. But, if one of you disagrees, there is no deal.

**TRAP**

Verbal offers are valueless. According to the Statute of Frauds, in order to be legally binding, offers for the purchase and sale of real estate must be in writing. Don't think you've got a deal when the buyer calls and tells you an offer over the phone and you accept. It's not a deal until everyone signs off.

## Counter When You Must

There's only one time to counter and that's when you can't accept the offer that's presented. In my opinion, you should almost never reject an offer flat out without a counter. To simply say no doesn't give the buyers an opening to come back. Maybe the first lowball offer was tentative on their part. They were just seeing if you were desperate enough to sell at a ridiculously low price. Now they're ready to come back with a higher offer. But if you don't counter, they may feel you're unwilling to budge at all, that you're being unreasonable and impossible to deal with. They may go elsewhere.

**TIP**

In a very hot market, some savvy sellers do reject offers for less than full price—sometimes even for full price! They're assuming that given the market, they should be able to get exactly what they are asking, or more, and the only way to convince a buyer of this is to give a flat-out rejection. I've seen this work, although you'd better be sure of your market before you try it.

A few years ago I was selling a small home in San Jose, California.

It was a rental property I owned long distance (usually a bad idea!) handled for me by a property management firm. I hadn't really seen it in a few years, although I did stop by just prior to putting it on the market to judge the condition and set a price that I thought was fairly reasonable.

I listed it with a local broker for a price of $315,000.

Almost two months later, the broker called to say that he had an offer. When I got together with the agents (a seller's broker, and a buyer's broker), I discovered that while the terms were acceptable, the offer was for $277,000, considerably less than I thought the property was worth.

The buyer's agent pointed out that this and that was wrong with the property; that it had been a rental and had been beaten up; and that $277,000 was all that it was worth. My seller's agent sat quietly and never commented. When I asked for his advice, he said, "Better take it. It's the first offer in nearly two months."

Both agents advocated my accepting the offer. However, having examined the market and the house, and knowing the comparables, I considered the offer frivolous. While the property might not bring the full $315,000 I was asking, it surely should bring something closer.

I was tempted to simply reject the offer out of hand, since the offering price and my asking price were so far apart that I was almost insulted. However, I concealed my feelings and instead, counteroffered. I countered at $310,000, just $5,000 less than my asking price.

My reasoning was that the offer might be frivolous, a way for someone to lowball me and steal the property for nothing. If that were the case, I would never hear from the buyers again. Alternatively, it might be a serious offer from a buyer who wanted to know how desperate I was to sell.

To my amazement, the buyer recountered at $305,000, up $28,000 from the previous offer and within $10,000 of my original asking price! I accepted.

The moral here is that you as a seller never know what buyers are thinking and unless you give buyers the benefit of the doubt with a counteroffer, you could be passing up an otherwise good deal.

## What Should You Counter On?

There are usually four areas in which you may want to make a counteroffer:

### Areas to Counter

Price
Terms
Occupancy
Contingencies

Remember, however, that if you make a counter in even just one of these areas, you've rejected the buyers' offer in all the rest. They may decide, on second thought, that they want to change some of the other areas or simply walk away.

## Countering the Price

Price is usually the number one concern for both buyers and sellers. Yes, you want and should get your price. Just remember, however, that the buyers feel the same way.

**TRAP**

Beware of a little game that sometimes occurs with offers. It's called "split the difference." In this game someone offers you less than you're asking. For example, you're asking $200,000 and they offer you $180,000. Since you had thought to get only $190,000 out of the deal anyhow, you decide to split the difference and counter at $190,000. Now, however, the buyers decide to split the difference again and they counter at $185,000. What are you going to do? If you split the difference again, you're going to counter at $187,500, less than you want. If you reject the offer flat out, you may lose the deal. Splitting the difference has done you in.

It's important not to reveal your rock-bottom price early on. If the buyers offer less than you're asking, perhaps you may want to counter at a price lower than you were originally asking, but still higher than your rock-bottom price so that you can have some maneuvering room. Don't just think of what you are offering. Play the game several moves ahead. What's going to happen after the next buyer's counteroffer?

## Countering the Terms

Terms might offer the greatest flexibility. Most often the buyers are seeking a new loan and plan to pay cash down to the loan. But many times they are asking you to carry part of the financing, perhaps a second or third mortgage for a portion of the down payment.

Just remember that everything is negotiable here. If you're willing to carry back some of the financing, you may agree to their proposed terms, but change the length of the loan or the interest rate. (The shorter the mortgage and the higher the interest rate, generally speaking, the better the deal for you.)

If you carry back "paper" (a second or lesser mortgage), try to see that it includes a monthly payment at least equal to the interest owed and that it also includes a *late penalty* for failure to make the payment on time. This will often make the mortgage more salable should you decide at a later date to cash it in.

## Countering the Occupancy

Although it seems a simple thing, I've seen many deals fall apart because of a disagreement over occupancy. You need to stay, the sellers need to get in, and neither will budge—the deal is lost.

If you want to sell your home, you have to be prepared to be flexible in terms of the timing. You have to be willing to give up on your schedule, if it means making the deal.

I've seen sellers move out early and live in a motel or rented house in order to make a deal. I've seen sellers stay six months longer than they planned (and pay rent to the buyers) because the buyers couldn't get in right away. I've even seen sellers give the buyers a bonus if they would agree to wait a few extra months before moving in.

There is really no reason an occupancy problem should ruin a deal, as long as you're flexible. Here are some alternatives:

### Solutions to Occupancy Problems

- Change your own time plans.
- Move and rent for a while.
- Stay and rent from the buyers.
- Pay the buyers a bonus to change their plans.
- Rent a motel suite for the buyers until you can move out.

Think of it this way: Is it worth a little inconvenience and/or money to you to sell your house?

## Countering on the Contingencies

In the counteroffer there are two ways to handle an unwanted contingency clause: the straightforward approach and the diplomatic approach.

You can be straightforward and simply cross out the contingency. You won't accept it. This states your position clearly, but it may offend the buyer and could cost you a deal.

**TIP**

A very successful builder friend had an absolute rule regarding contingencies: he refused to sign any agreement with a contingency in it, no matter how innocuous the clause was. He said it was just a way for the buyer to weasel out. It's something to consider.

On the other hand, you can be diplomatic and attempt to limit the contingency. The buyers have inserted a contingency which says that the purchase is subject to a great aunt coming down and approving the bedroom she'll be living in when the house is purchased.

Fine. You have no problem with that (although it sounds frivolous). Accept the contingency, only add that the great aunt has to give her approval within three days.

You haven't insulted the buyers. You haven't suggested that the contingency was a ploy to let them out of the deal. You've gone along with it. You've agreed to take your house off the market for three days while the buyers satisfy the great aunt or whomever.

But you've also made it clear that you mean business and that you don't have time for frivolous antics. After three days they either remove the contingency or they lose the house.

**TIP**

Time is the great limiter of contingencies.

The buyers say they want a structural engineer to examine your home to be sure that it wasn't damaged by the last earthquake. (Let's say you live in California.) Instead of simply saying no, you won't do that (which only makes the buyers suspicious), agree—provided that they pay the engineer and that they approve the inspection within a week.

Now you've limited the contingency by action and time.

Limiting the contingencies makes it appear that you're going along with the buyers' wishes, all the while making the offer more acceptable to you.

## Specify How a Contingency Is to Be Removed

If you're limiting a contingency by time, be sure that you specify how that contingency is to be removed. For example, the sellers want a soil inspection to check for drainage and flooding. You agree, but specify that they must provide you with written approval of a completed report within, for example, a week. Otherwise, the deal is off.

Also, remember that contingencies work both ways. There may come a time when you want to add a contingency to benefit you.

For example, the buyers want you to supply a termite clearance, which is pretty standard and usually a necessary part of getting a new loan. But you're afraid that there might be extensive termite damage. You don't mind spending a few thousand to clean up the termites, but you might balk at spending tens of thousands. Maybe you'd simply rather not sell in that event. You might write in a contingency that limits your costs in supplying the clearance to, say, $10,000.

If it's more than that amount, the deal's off. (Be sure that when you signed your listing agreement you didn't already agree to a termite clearance regardless of the costs.)

## What If the Buyers Walk?

What do you do when you've been too clever? The buyers made an offer and you countered at lower than your asking price, but higher than your rock-bottom price (hoping to pump a few more bucks out of the deal). You fully expected the buyers either to accept or to counter back. But instead, the buyers have done nothing!

Apparently they are simply rejecting your offer and looking elsewhere. Does that mean the deal is dead?

Not necessarily. There is nothing to keep you from making a second counteroffer even though the buyers have rejected the first and have not countered back.

Of course, it puts you in a rather weak position. You counter $166,000, for example, and when the buyers flat out refuse, you counter $164,000. It's bound to make the buyers wonder just how low you'll go if they just hang tight. Maybe your next counter will be for $160,000!

> **TIP**
>
> When you are making desperation counters, a good rule of thumb is to make only *one*.

Tell the buyers (through the agent, if possible) that you really want to sell and that you hoped that they would counter. However, since they didn't, you're going to make them one last, final offer—your very best deal, so to speak. Make it perfectly clear that this is your fallback position offer. If they don't take it, there won't be any others forthcoming.

Sometimes it works. Of course, it raises this question: What if the buyers now counter at a lower price or terms? (Selling real estate can be so aggravating!)

Ultimately, as always, you have to decide on the minimum for which you'll sell your property. You can't go any lower than you can go.

## How Do You Accept?

You don't have a deal until both parties sign the exact same sales agreement. For you, until the pen touches the paper with no changes, and actually for a short time afterward, there is no deal. Until you sign, you can refuse to accept the offer. (However, if the offer is for the price and terms you listed the property for, you could still be liable for a commission to the agent!)

It's important to understand, however, that the deal isn't made exactly when you sign. Rather, it's made when the agent (or you) communicates to the buyers the fact that you've signed. In practice, this means that usually the agent immediately calls the buyers to tell them you've accepted and then takes them a signed (by you) copy of the sales agreement. Technically speaking, the buyers can withdraw the offer anytime before they learn of your acceptance (just as you can withdraw a counteroffer anytime before the buyers accept it).

Sometimes the buyers (or you) are a long distance away. To facilitate the deal, the negotiations may be carried out over the phone. I've agreed to deals from thousands of miles away and then sent a copy of the signed agreement by either express mail or fax machine. Distances shouldn't keep a deal from happening.

## Always Keep Copies

The agent (or the buyers) must give you a copy of everything you sign. Be sure that you get that copy and that you hang onto it.

You can't say you've sold your house until the title is recorded and you've gotten your check, but at this stage, you can kick back and relax a bit. Hopefully, the hardest part is over.

To learn more about negotiating, try my book *Tips and Traps When Negotiating Real Estate* (McGraw-Hill, 2006).

# Dealing with a Bad Inspection Report

You've got a sale—you have a buyer and a signed purchase agreement. But when the inspection report on your property comes in, it notes all kinds of problems. The buyers are wary and threatening to pull out of the deal.

What can you do to save the sale?

## Why Let the Buyers Have an Inspection?

Today most buyers will insist on a professional home inspection as a condition of purchase. Should you as a seller oppose this, and avoid the problem noted above? Should you resist it? Should you attempt to negotiate your way out of it?

The answer is, "No!"

Buyers want the home inspection to protect themselves by uncovering any hidden problems. But savvy sellers want the inspection even more.

Why? Because it helps sellers protect themselves by showing that a serious effort has been made to discover any problems that might exist in the home. The buyers want an inspection. You tell them to go right ahead. After the sale, if a hidden problem turns up, you can point out that the buyers conducted their own professional inspection, which didn't discover the problem, so how could you disclose it? In short, the buyer's inspection helps cover *your* behind.

**TIP**

The buyers normally pay for their own professional inspection, typically around $300. So it shouldn't cost you anything for the inspection.

## Should You Have Your Home Professionally Inspected Prior to Sale?

It's a good idea for older homes. If you have the inspection conducted, you'll have to pay for it . . . and give the buyers a copy of the report. But it could save you a problem later on such as the one at the beginning of this chapter.

My feeling is that if you think your house is in great shape with no hidden problems, then don't bother with your own inspection. Let the buyers do it.

On the other hand, if you think there's a problem with the property or maybe you have a feeling some things may be wrong but you're not sure—or more importantly, if you have an older home—go ahead and do it yourself. The advantage of doing an inspection before the sale is that you can then select the method (and cost) of the fix. If the buyers conduct an inspection and find something wrong, they may demand it be fixed at a much greater cost—or back out of the deal.

**TRAP**

Most inspectors are gun-shy these days. They are wary of missing something and having buyers or sellers come back at them later. As a consequence, they fill their report with so many disclaimers (and sometimes do such a cursory job) that sometimes the report is almost useless.

## What Do You Do with a Bad Inspection Report?

Okay, let's get down to the nitty-gritty. The buyers pay for an inspection and it shows that the wiring in the house is faulty. Or the plumbing is leaking. Or the roof has holes in it. Or the foundation is cracked. Or any number of other big-ticket items. What do you do?

Here's the procedure to follow when you get a bad professional inspection report:

### 10 Ways to Respond to a Bad Inspection Report

1. **Get a copy of the report and read it carefully.** It may not actually be as bad as your agent first said.
2. **Find out how the buyers responded.** In the worst case, they walked away from the deal. But more likely, they want to know if you'll fix the problem and probably will go forward with the deal if you do.
3. **Find out how much a fix will cost.** Don't rely on an estimate from the home inspector. There could be a conflict of interest. Get at least three independent estimates if the cost is going to be over $1,000. (You may want to go with the lowest since you're moving out of the home anyway.) Also, consider if you want and can do the fix yourself.
4. **Agree to deal with the problem.** Assume you can't sell to this buyer or any other until the problem is handled, so you have to bite the bullet and go forward.

5. **Aim for repairs rather than replacement.** If the roof leaks, you'll have it repaired, not replaced. If the foundation is cracked, you'll have it repaired, not replaced. Get the buyer to sign off on this.

6. **Compromise with an adamant buyer.** The buyer insists on replacement of the roof or foundation, not repairs. The buyer says the damage or wear is too great. The lowest estimate is $25,000. Tell the buyer that to save the deal, you'll pay half as a credit to the buyer in escrow, if the buyer will pay the other half. (After all, the buyers get the full benefit of the work since they are moving in—you get none since you're moving out.)

7. **Consider refusing.** The buyer wants the roof replaced, but won't pay for any of it. Perhaps it's time to walk away from the deal. The next buyer may be more reasonable.

8. **Get the work done.** After the buyer has signed off on your repair or replacement plans, get the work done.

9. **Get the buyer to approve the work.** This is the reason you want the buyers to sign off on what's to be done, or else they might disapprove of what you've done and you might have to do it over. (Don't laugh. I once had to redo an entire deck because the buyers didn't like the shade of redwood color I had chosen!)

10. **Finish the deal.** There's almost always a way to handle a problem that's been revealed by a professional inspection, provided both buyer and seller are willing to work together on it.

**TRAP**

Getting big work done before putting the house on the market may save you money. But it may also mean you'll do a job that a future buyer might not like.

## How Do You Get a Good Inspector?

These days most inspectors advertise in the Yellow Pages, in newspapers, and online. However, be aware that as of this writing, inspectors are not yet licensed in all states. Ask for recommendations from agents. Most agents know one or two inspectors whom they rely upon and trust.

Ask the inspector you're considering for a couple of references. Then call these people. Chances are the inspection was made a few months ago and they've already moved in. Did they find that the inspector missed anything? Were they otherwise satisfied?

Be sure the inspector belongs to a national trade organization such as:

> International Association of Certified Home Inspectors
> (www.nachi.org)
> American Society of Home Inspectors
> (www.ashi.com)
> National Association of Home Inspectors
> (www.nahi.org)

Recently contractors, particularly those who haven't had much luck in building, have taken to house inspections as a way of raising additional money. A contractor can walk through your house, put checks on a form, and pick up several hundred dollars for a few hours work. Also, if there's a problem, the contractor can then recommend his or her own company for the repair work. It's not surprising that many are doing so.

But are contractors qualified? Some are and some aren't. A contractor who builds houses new may not know a great deal about old houses. A plumbing contractor may not know about electrical. A cement contractor may know very little about roofs. The value of their inspections may be questionable.

I like an inspector who has a general knowledge plus a degree in one or more property related fields, such as soils engineering. Retired city building and safety department inspectors are often good choices.

## What Should You Have the Inspector Check?

**TRAP**

Normally, inspectors will not render an opinion on any area that's not easily accessible. This often includes floors under carpeting, inside walls, inaccessible roofs, and so on. Each of the organizations noted above offers a "standards of practice" that describes what its inspectors should do when they go through your home.

There are many areas of the home that sellers should be aware of and that should be inspected either by you or by a competent inspector. These include, but are not limited to, the following:

### Areas That Should Be Inspected

1. **Fireplace and fireplace exhaust.** Loose bricks, blockage, chimney lining
2. **Electrical system.** Circuit breakers, wall receptacles, switches, wiring, light fixtures, adequacy of grounding
3. **Heating/cooling system.** Combustion chamber, cleanliness of heater, blockages, compression in air conditioners, motors
4. **Plumbing.** Type of pipe and age, rusting, leaks, water disposal condition, water pressure (too high or too low)
5. **Sewerage, septic tank, and other waste disposal.** Leakage, breakage, blockage
6. **Foundation and structure.** Cracks, breaks, leaning, flooding in basement
7. **Additions made without building department approval.** Room additions, window or door changes, addition of electric or gas appliances

8. **Exterior and roof.** Age of exterior and roof and condition, gutters and downspouts, cracking of stucco, peeling of paint

9. **Doors and windows (including leakage).** Weather stripping, hinges, alignment

10. **Drainage and flooding.** Slope, groundwater conditions, drainage away from house

11. **Interior.** Condition of walls, ceilings, carpets, and drapes

12. **Lot.** Safety of fences and gates, any obstructions

13. **Appliances.** Age and condition

Beware of contractors who offer to do a home inspection for a nominal fee, then find something wrong and offer to fix it, usually for a high fee. A few unscrupulous contractors have been using home inspection as a way of procuring business for themselves. A good rule of thumb is not to have the work done by the same person who does the inspection. (Also, don't ask the inspector to refer you to someone. That someone could be the inspector's brother-in-law or sister.)

It should go without saying that you should always insist on a written report. However, in truth, accompanying the inspector on the inspection, asking questions, and getting answers, may prove the most useful of all.

## Should You Have a Termite Inspection?

Termite (and other pest) inspections are not really a new part of the home inspection process. Lenders have been requiring termite inspections as a condition for approving a new home loan for decades. A termite inspection and the repair of damage have been requirements of home sales for almost as long a time. In almost all states termite inspectors are licensed and their written reports must be registered.

Usually the seller pays for the termite inspection and for correction of any damages. The buyer usually pays to have any preventive work.

Thus, while there may be little advantage of doing a termite inspection before you catch a buyer (unless you are worried about a particular problem), in an older house it probably can't hurt to have it ready to go, either. Just be wary of paying for a termite inspection only to find that the house doesn't get sold. The termite inspection is only good for a limited time, typically 90 days. If you don't sell within the time period, you'll probably need to get, and pay for, a new inspection.

## Should You Pay for a Buyer's Home Warranty Plan?

In addition to an inspection, you can obtain a home warranty, which covers the major systems (heating, electrical, plumbing) as well as appliances. A typical home warranty plan usually costs about $300 a year with the seller paying the first year of it. It covers problems that occur after you move out and the buyer moves in.

It can be money well spent. If minor (and sometimes major) problems crop up, the warranty often covers them, instead of you. Thus, if a water heater goes out, the buyers don't come running to you for a fix. They contact the warranty company.

Almost all agents can put you in touch with a salesperson for a home warranty company in your area. Also check the Internet:

www.americanhomeshield.com
www.nationwidehomewarranty.com
www.libertyhomeprotection.com

# What to Say on Your Disclosures

f you haven't been exposed to disclosures before, you almost certainly will as you sell your home today. Most states now require them, and most buyers demand them: a written list disclosing any defects with the home. You'll need to write out that list.

For many sellers, this can be a shock. "You mean I have to report about that leak in the roof . . . or that crack in the foundation? Why, it might mean the buyer will back out of the deal—or offer less!"

Yep, you have to report the roof leak and the foundation crack and a whole lot more. And indeed, it could require renegotiating the sale, although it will probably not ruin the deal. That's why it's a good idea to present the disclosures to buyers up front, right when they are presenting their offer, so there aren't any hidden problems that could come up later.

## Do You Have to Disclose Everything?

I can remember back not so many years ago that when sellers listed their properties, the first thing they did was cover up all the problems. Holes in the foundation were spackled, cracks in walls painted over, a few new shingles placed where water leaked in, a temporary fix put on a bulging water pipe, and so on. The idea was to sell the buyers on the concept that the house was in great shape. Once buyers bought and found out otherwise, it was their problem. Caveat emptor—let the buyer beware.

Times have changed enormously. Complaints and lawsuits by buyers against sellers (and their agents) have turned things around 180 degrees. Today savvy sellers know that if there's a problem with the house that they fail to disclose, and the buyers later find out about it, the sellers might not only have to pay to have the problem corrected (usually in the most expensive way). In an extreme case, sellers might even have to give the buyers back their money and take back the house!

Nobody wants that sort of thing to happen. When you sell your house, you want it to stay sold. And you don't want to be replacing expensive items for the buyers later on. You want a clean deal.

To get a clean deal, you must disclose what's wrong with the property. Some even argue that you must disclose what you should know is wrong with the property, even if you don't know it!

All of which is to say that today disclosure is a big part of selling. As noted, most states today require that sellers give buyers a formal disclosure statement, and some even prescribe the basics of what goes into that statement. (Check with your agent to see what the rules are in your state.)

But even if the state doesn't tell you what you should disclose, you should prepare your own disclosure statement and give it to the buyer, if for no other reason than to protect yourself.

Remember, if you tell the buyer the house has a cracked foundation and the buyer goes ahead with the purchase anyhow, what's that buyer got to complain about later on?

TIP

My own philosophy in selling properties that I own is to disclose everything, in great detail, no matter how small the problem appears to be. This has a big advantage in that I seldom have to worry about buyers coming back at me later on claiming I didn't tell them about something. It's all out in the open. If there's a problem, it's dealt with at the time of sale.

## What's the Worst That Could Happen If You Don't Disclose?

Disclosure is not something to take lightly. I recently had occasion to witness a confrontation among sellers, buyers, and agents that would most certainly not have taken place 10 years earlier.

The situation was quite simple on the face of it.

The buyers had purchased a single-family home in what appeared to be a nice neighborhood. They had paid close to asking price and the deal went smoothly. At the closing, buyers, sellers, and agent all seemed satisfied. The deed was recorded in favor of the buyers, the sellers received their cash out, and the agent her commission.

About two weeks later, the buyers called the seller's agent (there were two involved in the transaction ) and complained that there was a severe problem with the home.

The next-door neighbors had a teenage daughter and son.

The kids would play their stereo loud during the day and then have parties two or three times a week until early in the morning.

The buyers weren't able to sleep or to enjoy their property. They said they had talked to the neighbors, all to no avail.

The agent chuckled and said that kids would be kids and to ignore it. If it got really bad, they should call the cops.

A week later the agent got another phone call. The buyers had called the police, who indicated that there wasn't much they could (or were willing to) do and revealed that the former owners (the sellers) had frequently called to complain about the same thing.

The buyers said they were thinking about demanding a recision of the deal. This caught the agent's attention. Recision essentially means to go back in time until all the parties are where they were before the deal was made. In other words, it means to take back the sale of the property.

The agent investigated and talked to the former sellers. The neighbors had indeed been a big problem. That, it turns out, was the real reason they had decided to sell! They had filed numerous police reports against those neighbors.

"But," the agent protested, "why didn't you tell me about that? Why didn't you tell the buyers?"

"Because," came the reply, "who would have bought the house if we'd mentioned it?"

The agent suspected she was in big trouble. She went to see the neighbors, who were intransigent. They refused to curb their children.

She went to see the buyers, who had dark hollows under their eyes and who were in the process of contacting an attorney. They couldn't sleep, and if they couldn't sleep they weren't getting the "quiet enjoyment" they were entitled to from their home. The agent had to agree.

The buyers did get an attorney and did pursue the matter, although it never got to court. By then it became evident that in their state, the sellers' duty to disclose defects in the house to buyers was clear. The sellers should have disclosed that there were problems with the neighbors.

How was the issue resolved? In the end, the agent negotiated with the noisy neighbors to sell their home!

It could have been much worse for the sellers. The buyers might have insisted on recision, in which case the sellers might have had to pay back all the buyers' money and take back the house!

And it was all over noisy neighbors, something that wasn't directly a part of the house that was sold.

In recent years sellers have been held liable for a whole raft of potential drawbacks to a property that a decade ago would never have caused a raised eyebrow. These include:

### Unusual Problems That Should Be Disclosed

- A death or murder in the house being sold
- A landfill nearby
- Flooding, grading, or drainage problems
- Zoning violations
- Soil problems
- Bad neighbors

All of which is to say that if you don't disclose any and all problems with your property, the consequences could be severe.

## It's What You Should Know

"But," you may be saying to yourself, "those sellers in the example withheld information. I would never do that. I would simply reveal everything I knew about the house." Unfortunately, it's like getting a traffic ticket. Ignorance of the law is no excuse. It's not always what you know and disclose to the buyers that counts. It's what you should have known and should have disclosed.

Much of the disclosure precedent came from a lawsuit in California (*Easton v. Strassburger*, A010566, California First District Court of Appeal, February 1984). The results of this lawsuit were codified in California law and subsequently in the real estate codes of many other states. The California real estate code deals primarily with the agent's responsibilities. It states: "An agent's duty to prospective purchasers of residential property of one to four units is: to state that he or she has conducted a reasonably competent and diligent visual inspection of the listed property and to disclose all facts revealed that materially affect the value or desirability of the property."

With regard to the sellers, the rules can be similar. The sellers often must disclose to the buyers any defects in the property that would materially affect its value or desirability—after they have conducted a reasonable inspection.

If you don't know, a part of the answer is to have your home inspected. You can either conduct an inspection yourself or hire a competent inspector (discussed in Chapter 14) to do it for you. Most sellers rely on the professional inspection that the buyers conduct and pay for.

**TRAP**

Most of the problems with a home—that a seller doesn't know anything about—deal with systems like plumbing, heating, electrical, gas, and so on, as well as structure. You might live in a house for 10 years and have occasionally smelled gas, but be otherwise unaware that a problem in the gas system exists. A buyer could purchase the home and it might blow up the next week. It could be argued that the gas system should have been checked.

## Do You Have to Fix Problems You Disclose?

While you must disclose problems and defects in your home, you don't necessarily have to fix them. Of course, if they are a safety hazard and liability issue, you will almost certainly want to see them fixed.

For example, your lot could have a perennial drainage problem. Every winter the storms in the nearby hills drop several inches of rain that floods your backyard. The flooding lasts for about a week and then drains away. You could fully disclose the problem to the buyers, yet they could opt to still purchase the house with the existing condition. You wouldn't have to fix it.

Or you could be near a landfill that occasionally produces noxious smells. As long as the buyer is made fully aware of the problem and agrees to buy the house with it, you're probably okay. (What, for example, could you do about correcting the landfill's odors?)

On the other hand, an inspection reveals a shorted light switch. You ignore it and the first time the buyer turns on the light, she's electrocuted. Shouldn't you have fixed that switch?

Of course, deciding what should and should not be fixed requires the wisdom of Solomon. But one thing is clear. The more you disclose to a buyer, the less chance there is for you to have trouble later on. And the more you fix health and safety issues, the less chance there is of someone getting hurt.

**TRAP**

Some sellers and their agents have taken to selling homes on an "as is" basis in the hopes of getting around the disclosure dilemma. This simply does not work. Asking buyers to take a property "as is" does not negate the need to disclose problems. Oh, you *can* ask the buyers to take the house "as is," but only after you've disclosed all the problems and the buyers know what they are getting and agree to accept them.

## When Should You Disclose?

As I've said, my feeling is the sooner the better. It's important to understand that to avoid any possibility of problems, you should disclose defects or problems with your house as soon as possible. That can mean even *before* the buyer makes an offer. In other words, if you're using an agent, the agent could present your disclosure sheet to the buyer before accepting an offer. If you're handling the house yourself, you could present it to the buyer before accepting any money or signing any sales agreement.

The idea is that the more you get out on the table before the sale, the less you have to worry about afterward. Be sure that the disclosure sheet is made at least in duplicate and that you retain a copy signed and dated by the buyers stating that they have seen and had a chance to read it.

**TRAP**

If you hold off showing the disclosure sheet until after the buyer makes an offer you accept, the buyer may have the right to take back the offer once the disclosure is given. That could negate the sale or start negotiations all over again.

## Should You Fix the Problem?

As noted, the downside of disclosing a problem is that it may cause a buyer to walk away. Or to make a much lower offer.

The solution here is to confront the problem out in the open and deal with it. There are two ways to do this: You can either fix the problem or give the buyers a cash discount because of it.

The most common example I know of has to do with leaking roofs. You, the seller, disclose that your roof leaks. The buyers understandably don't want to buy a house with a leaky roof.

You can do one of two things. Before you put the house on the market, fix the roof. If the roof is basically in good shape, but just has a few leaks, it won't be that expensive a repair. Then, you can disclose that the roof used to have leaks, but that now it doesn't because you had it fixed.

Or, if the roof is in terrible shape and must be replaced, you can offer the buyers a discount. I like the discount idea because there are many kinds of roofs and the buyers may want a more expensive (or less expensive) roof than you would choose.

**TRAP**

If you disclose a bad roof and offer a discount to the buyers, the lender may require that the roof be replaced before funding the mortgage. (The lender may fear the buyer won't do the work and if it had to foreclose, it would take back a house with a bad roof.) If this is the case, you may have no choice but to go ahead and replace it yourself.

At least consult with the buyers so you don't do work with materials that they hate and that will cause them to back out of the deal or demand that you redo the work.

## Mandatory Federal Disclosures

In addition to state required disclosures, the federal government also requires disclosures with regard to lead. You must give the buyer a specific statement regarding your knowledge of the presence (or absence) of any lead in the paint or on the property. You must also provide them with a special booklet which describes the dangers of lead poisoning. Your agent should help you with this. Or you can get the form and the booklet via the Internet. (Check out www.hud.gov.)

## Disclosure Sheets

To help sellers with their disclosures, agents and some real estate associations have created their own disclosure sheet forms. (If you're not using an agent, you can usually get a copy from an agent.) These are given to prospective buyers and they help the sellers organize their disclosures. Here's what a typical disclosure statement might contain. (*Note:* Check with an agent/attorney first to see if a different disclosure statement must be used in your area.)

## Typical Disclosure Statement

*Occupancy:* Who is occupying the property? If it's a tenant, will there be any difficulties in getting possession?

*Appliances and features contained on the property* (note that the following is only a partial checklist):

| | |
|---|---|
| Oven | Trash compactor |
| Range | Microwave |
| Dishwasher | Washer/dryer hookups |
| Sewer | Septic tank |
| TV antenna | Security system |
| Well | Wall air conditioners |
| Sprinklers | Solar heating |
| Gutters | Fire alarm |
| Intercom | Gazebo |
| Spa | Carport |
| Garage | Garage door opener |
| Pool | Heater/filter |
| Window screens | Satellite dish |
| Exhaust fan | Garbage disposal |
| Fireplace | 220-volt wiring |

*Roof:* Age, type, and condition

*Defects or problem areas in the house:*

| | |
|---|---|
| Interior walls | Exterior walls |
| Ceilings | Floors |
| Roof | Insulation |
| Windows | Doors |

| | |
|---|---|
| Foundation | Slab |
| Driveway | Sidewalk |
| Fences | Gates |
| Electrical | Plumbing |
| Sewer | Heating/cooling |
| Structure | |

*Other problem areas:*

1. Is there a homeowners association?
2. Are there any common areas? Describe them.
3. Are there any lawsuits that might affect the property?
4. Any deed restrictions or other CC&R restrictions?
5. Any bond obligations (such as a bond to pay for a sewer connection)?
6. Any zoning or setback violations?
7. Any damage to the property from fires?
8. Any damage from flooding or earthquakes?
9. Any settling or soil slippage?
10. Any room additions made without a building permit?
11. Any encroachments from neighboring properties?
12. Any easements?
13. Any landfill on the property?
14. Any common fences or driveways shared with neighbors?
15. Any other problems with the property?

# How to Legally Avoid Paying Taxes on the Sale

The good news is that real estate offers you an enormous tax break when it comes time to sell your home. It allows you to exclude (not pay) taxes on up to $500,000 of your capital gain (if you're married, file jointly, and meet the rules). Where else are you going to find a tax break like that?

All of which is to say that if you're contemplating selling your house, you would be wise to first look at the tax laws. By timing your sale and structuring it just right, you could save yourself a pile of money that you'd otherwise end up paying in taxes.

> **NOTE** The author is not engaged in providing tax advice. The following is an overview of tax rules generally affecting real estate, hence you should not rely on it for your specific property. For tax advice, consult with a tax professional.

Under the 1997 Taxpayer Relief Act, each person regardless of age can exclude up to $250,000 of the capital gain on the sale of a principle residence. For a couple filing jointly, that multiplies to $500,000.

Will you have a gain on your sale?

Even where prices have gone down on properties, often there is a gain, particularly if you bought your property years ago when prices were much, much lower. (Later in this chapter, we'll discuss what happens when you lose money on the sale.)

Normally, if you have a gain on the sale, you owe taxes on that gain. Gain is calculated as the difference between your adjusted basis and your net selling price. The actual calculation can be tricky and should be made by a tax specialist.

As suggested, much of the tax planning for a sale of a personal residence revolves around being sure that you qualify for the up to $500,000 exclusion (for married couples filing jointly). Obviously, being able to exclude up to $500,000 of the gain can make a big difference in your tax liability. And for most people it's a highly desirable option. (I say "most" because for some wealthy taxpayers whose gain is substantially more than the maximum, other alternatives, such as converting to a rental and subsequently doing a tax-deferred exchange may be an option.)

There are some basic rules that must be followed in order to qualify for the exclusion.

## Basic Rules

- The home must be your principal residence—you must own and actually occupy it.
- You must have lived in the property for two out of the previous five years.
- You can only take the exclusion once every two years.

While the basics are fairly simple, there are many circumstances that come close, but do not quite fit the formula. Before considering these, however, let's take a quick look at what this law changed.

## No Rollover Required

There were many tax planning rules prior to the 1997 change in the tax code, and unfortunately many people still think they apply. Here are some that are no longer applicable:

### No Deferral

In the past, you had to purchase another property of the same or greater value in order to defer gain. At that time it was not an *exclusion* but a *deferral*. Your gain was deferred into the future and into the new property.

Today, that's no longer the case. You do not have to buy another property and defer the gain into it.

### No Need to Buy Another Property

Further, the money that you take out of the property need not be reinvested in any real estate. You can do with it as you wish: take a holiday, gamble it away in Vegas, or give it to your children.

### Eased Reporting

In the past, the home sale had to be reported on IRS Form 2119 (sale of your home). That was eliminated a year after the new rules took effect. Generally speaking, if your gain does not exceed the $250,000 per person or $500,000 per married couple filing jointly, you do not need to report the sale to the feds. If the gain exceeds these amounts, then you need to report it on IRS Form 1040, Schedule D to the federal government, and as your state requires.

### Don't Have to Move a Certain Number of Miles

You do not have to move a certain distance, for example 50 miles, away from your old home in order to qualify for the exclusion.

### No Age Requirement

In the past, the rule applied only if you were aged 55 or older. That provision has been repealed. You do not need to reach a minimum age in order to qualify.

### No "Once in a Lifetime" Provision

The fact that you previously took the exclusion under the old rules in no way precludes you from taking it again under the new rules. In effect, you get it back.

## New Rules

To qualify, the house must be your principal residence. That means that it must be your "main house." Often it means simply where you spend the majority of your time. If you have two houses (a second vacation home, for example) your principal residence is often determined by many factors including:

### It's Your Principal Residence If . . .

- It's near where your work.
- It's where you and your family reside.

- It's where you are registered to vote.
- It's the address you use when sending in your federal and state tax returns and it's the mailing address for bills.
- Other factors indicating you live there.

You must also live in it for a minimum of two out of five years. That means that if you moved in yesterday, it will be two years before you can claim the exclusion. (There are some extenuating circumstances which we'll discuss shortly.)

From a tax planning standpoint, assuming you make a profit on your house, it's therefore likely to be to your advantage to remain in the home at least two years before selling it.

## What If You Don't Live There Continuously?

While you may plan on residing in your home right now, your circumstances may change in the future. You may find that you need to move away because of a job change, change in your marital situation, health, or for any number of other reasons. Rather than sell the property, you may opt to rent it out. Renting it will not preclude claiming the exclusion, provided the required years lived in are met.

Remember, you must have resided in the property for two out of the previous five years. That means that you can rent the property out for three out of the previous five years. Furthermore, the periods of occupancy and renting do not have to be continuous. You could live in it for year, rent it out for three years and then come back and live in it for one year, thus meeting the requirement.

### Extended Vacations?

It's okay to take temporary vacations. But it depends on the circumstances. For example, if you take a cruise that lasts a month, it is undoubtedly a temporary vacation and shouldn't affect your occupancy status with regard to the home.

On the other hand, if you move to another country for 13 months it's a different story. Even if you don't rent the property out during that time, the IRS might not consider your move "temporary."

## Two Unmarried Owners?

Then each one must independently qualify for the maximum limitation. Each will file separate returns, report the gains, and may claim up to the $250,000 exclusion.

## One Spouse Qualifies?

This opens a whole can of worms. For example, it is possible for each spouse to have his or her separate principal residence. If that's the case, then each could potentially qualify for the up to $250,000 exclusion on his or her property, provided each meets the basic requirements.

Or, if both spouses own the property, but only one has occupied it for two years (as when there is a marriage and one member previously owned the house), then only the spouse who has occupied it for two years might claim the exclusion.

## Are There Exceptions to the Rule?

Even though you fully intend to meet the guidelines of the exclusion rule, circumstances may prevent you from doing so. If that's the case, then you may still be able to claim at least a part, if not all, of the amount.

### Possible Exceptions to the Rule

- **Employment issues.** You might lose your current job and find another one far away. If the move is more than 50 miles away, you might be forced to sell your home and could challenge the two-out-of-five-year rule.
- **Health issues.** You may contract an illness or have an accident which necessitates your moving from the house.
- **Unforeseen issues.** Generally speaking, you will need to establish that the primary reason for the sale was unanticipated. This is usually on a case-by-case basis but might include condemnation of the house or breakup of a couple that intended to get married.

**TIP**

Don't assume anything. A lot of the exceptions to the exclusion are determined on a case by case basis. Check with a good tax professional first.

If you have a qualified exception, then you may get at least a partial exclusion. Generally speaking, this is determined by one of two formulas. Either you divide the days of use into two years (730 days) or the days between the sale of your last home which qualified for the exclusion and the current sale into two years. Whichever is less is taken as a percentage, which then applies to the up to $500,000 exclusion for a couple filing jointly. If, for example, you had a qualified exception, hadn't previously taken the exclusion, and you occupied your principal residence for six months, you would probably end up with a quarter of the exclusion amount.

## Other Tax Issues Affected Upon Sale

### How Are Your Property Tax Deductions Handled When You Sell?

Generally speaking, while you own the property you can deduct the amount you pay in property taxes from your federal and, in most cases, your state income taxes.

However, that ends on the day the escrow closes and the property title transfers to the buyers. Therefore, as part of the escrow process, property taxes are usually prorated. That means that you pay right up to the close of escrow and the buyers pay from there. It's seen as an adjustment on your closing statement.

Be sure to save that closing statement and take it to your accountant when he or she does your taxes. From it, your accountant will be able to determine exactly how much money in taxes you are able to deduct in the year of sale.

## What About the Interest on Your Mortgage When You Sell?

Generally speaking, mortgage interest—up to certain limits—is deductible while you own the property and when the mortgage is in your name. The limitations include:

1. The maximum mortgage amount deducted can be $1 million, provided that the mortgage was used to purchase, build, or improve your home.
2. The deduction applies only to your principal residence and to a second home. If it's a second home, you must use it part of the year.
3. Any mortgage debt taken out prior to October 13, 1987, is grandfathered in.
4. If you take out a mortgage on (refinance) your home for purposes other than to improve, build, or add on, you are limited to $100,000 of debt on which interest may be deducted.

The rule is tricky. You may purchase a home with a mortgage of $450,000. Under the rule, all of the interest on this mortgage is presumably deductible. After you buy the property, you decide to add to the house and secure a mortgage for $150,000 more. If the money is used to build or improve the property, all the interest on the second mortgage is probably deductible.

However, if you took out a second on the same property for $150,000 and used the money to start a business of your own, only the interest on the first $100,000 of the debt likely would be deductible.

Also, if you take out a mortgage against your home and then buy bonds that are tax free or otherwise receive tax free income, the interest on the mortgage may not be deductible.

On the other hand, there may be a special exception available to you if you use the money for education.

When you sell your property, generally speaking, all of the interest you are allowed to deduct continues on until the close of escrow. Presumably at the time, your mortgages are paid off, hence, there are no further interest deductions you can take. If the interest were to continue, then the loans would presumably not be secured by real estate, but would be personal. And interest on personal loans in general is not deductible.

Be sure to see a good accountant in the year you sell your home to help you determine what interest you can deduct.

## Are the Points You Paid When You Bought Your Home Deductible When You Sell?

Maybe.

Points are usually a form of prepaid interest. These are paid up front when you get the loan. Points are often deductible, but not necessarily all in the same year.

If the points truly represent prepaid interest, then you may deduct them. However, you must usually deduct them over the life of the mortgage. If the mortgage is for 30 years, then the deduction for points must be spread out over that period. For example, two points on a $200,000 mortgage for 30 years are deductible at $133 a year. (We'll get back to this in a few moments.)

Some points, however, are deductible in the year you buy the house.

### You Can Deduct Points in the Year You Purchase the House If . . .

- The mortgage must be for your principal residence. It must be used for buying or improving that residence. You cannot deduct points in the year paid on a mortgage for a second residence, even though interest on that mortgage may be deductible. You may, however, be able to deduct the points over the life of the mortgage on the second home.

  Your principal residence is generally the place where you spend most of your time. Unless you spend more than 50 percent of your time there, it might be hard to prove that a house was your principal residence.

- You should generally pay the points out of your own funds. The points are not paid out of the money loaned to you by the lender. This issue comes into play when the lender rolls your closing costs into the mortgage. Many buyers pay points with a separate check to help define their use.

- The amount of points charged must be customary for the area. If you "buy down" a mortgage (by paying additional points up front), the government may determine that the points you paid were in excess of what is customary for your area and disallow the deduction in the year paid.

- The points cannot be the fees paid for appraisals, credit reports or the origination fees charged for FHA loans or special fees charged for VA loans.

- The points must represent interest. The deductions are applicable only if the points do not exceed the maximum interest deduction allowable on a residence.

Finally, to answer the initial question about deducting points in the year of sale: if qualified as noted above and you deducted your points when you bought the property, you obviously cannot deduct them a second time when you sell. However, if you spread out your points over the life of the mortgage and then paid the mortgage off at the time you sold, you may be able to then deduct those remaining points at the time of sale.

Again, check with a good accountant who can give you an answer to your specific situation.

## What If You Have a Loss on the Sale?

Generally speaking, if you instead of having a capital gain when you sell your home, you have a capital loss, you cannot take a deduction for that loss if the property was your principal residence. This is a quirk in the tax rules long railed about by many homeowners who have lost money on their properties.

As of this writing, there is a movement in Congress to change the tax rules to allow at least some deduction for a tax loss on the sale of your main residence. Check with an accountant to see what the rules are at the time you sell.

## What If You Have a Short Sale and Some of Your Mortgage Is Forgiven by the Lender?

This is a more complex subject than most people realize. Generally speaking, the IRS has said that an amount on a mortgage that is forgiven in a short sale with a short payoff may be considered income. Therefore, if when you sell your home on a short sale, you could be liable for taxes on the amount that is forgiven!

This sometimes comes as a huge shock to sellers who have gotten out from under an "underwater" property in a short sale. They suddenly realize that they could potentially owe taxes on the forgiven amount of their mortgage.

However, in talking to several tax specialists, the interpretation I have heard is that the rule does not apply to all mortgages. In other words, it may only apply to mortgages that you put on the property *not* as part of the purchase price. For purchase money mortgages in a short sale, the forgiven amount might not be characterized as taxable. Only if you refinanced or put a second mortgage on your property might the forgiven amount of the mortgage be taxable.

Further, the Forgiveness Debt Relief Act provides that up to $2 million of forgiven debt is federal income tax free. It's for the years 2007 to 2009. The exclusion only affects those who obtained a mortgage on their principal residence for the purpose of construction or renovation.

All of which is to say, this subject is complex and should be interpreted by a tax professional. Be sure to consult one if you have a short sale.

## Importance of Record Keeping

Most people have no idea what their gain (or loss) is when they sell. Homes purchased as little as five years ago in some areas of the country have shot up in value. And then shot down.

To be safe, you should keep records that will affect the tax basis of your property. Who knows? When it comes time to sell, you may find that your gain is more than the $250,000 for individuals or $500,000 limit for married couples filing jointly or you otherwise don't qualify for the exclusion—and you would have tax to pay.

However, if you've kept records of your home improvements, your basis could be adjusted upwards. Then you may find you actually don't owe as much in taxes, or any at all.

Always keep good records.

## What If You Rent Out Your House Instead of Selling?

In earlier chapters we spoke of alternatives to selling; for example, the lease option and the rental. How do taxes affect you if you're in this situation? (For the remainder of this chapter, we will assume you're renting out your home.)

If you own and rent investment real estate, normally you can depreciate it. Depreciating means taking a certain percentage of its "cost" (we'll talk more about this later) each year as a reduction in value.

Almost all business assets can be depreciated. Cars, for example, are depreciated over a lifespan of five years. In a straight-line method, you might take 20 percent a year of the cost as a loss of value.

Residential real estate must be depreciated over 27.5 years. Again, using a straight-line method you would take $1/_{27.5}$ of the cost each year as a loss in value.

Of course, the value of property sometimes goes up, not down. So, how you can take a loss on an asset that's increasing in value? A helpful way to understand this is to think of it is as a "paper loss." All assets deteriorate over time. Even a house will eventually fall away to dust. So instead of simply waiting until the end of its useful lifespan (arbitrarily decided by the government), you take a portion of the loss in value each year.

But, you may reasonably note, while the house will eventually deteriorate, the land never will. How do you depreciate land costs?

The answer is you can't. You can only depreciate the building, not the land. The only exceptions would be if the land itself had an asset that was depletable, such as gas and oil, and that's not the case here.

## Is Depreciation an Expense?

Yes, it is. It's an expense much in the way you have other expenses when you own rental property. For example, here's a list of some expenses you might expect to incur:

### Typical Rental Property Expenses

- Mortgage interest
- Taxes
- Insurance
- Water service
- Garbage service
- Maintenance and repair
- Fix-up
- Advertising
- Pool and garden service
- Depreciation

**TIP**

Unlike owning a house, in which you live where the only deductions are typically property taxes and mortgage interest, with a rental property almost everything is deductible. You may be able to deduct a phone, auto, even business cards! Check with your accountant.

When you add up all of the above expenses, you have the total expenses for your property over a month. Add all the monthlies together and that's how much it costs you over a year.

Now, subtract your total annual expenses from your total annual income, and that's your profit or loss.

## Does Depreciation Contribute to Loss, at Least on Paper?

It certainly does. Even if you should be so fortunate as to find a property that breaks even (or makes a small profit), as soon as you add the paper loss of depreciation to your cash expenses, you almost always find that there's a loss.

### Typical Income/Expense on a Rental House

| | |
|---|---|
| Total annual income | $14,400 ($1,200 monthly) |
| Total annual cash expenses | −14,000 |
| Positive cash flow | 400 |
| Annual depreciation | −7,500 |
| Annual loss | −7,100 |

Once depreciation is added in, you can almost always be assured that the property will show a loss, at least on paper. In our above example, a good property that actually shows a positive cash flow (more money coming in than cash expenses going out) turns into a big loser as soon as depreciation is added.

**TIP**

Remember that the loss from depreciation is not an out-of-pocket expense. It's an accounting loss—it shows up on paper.

In the distant past, depreciation was a tax dodge that was used by the wealthy to reduce their sizable incomes. They would take that loss from real estate (that only occurred on paper) and deduct it from their ordinary income. That reduced their ordinary income and, of course, reduced the amount of taxes they would owe on that income.

That tax shelter was eliminated for the wealthy by the Tax Reform Act of 1986. Now it is only available if your income is less than $150,000. We'll have more to say about this shortly.

## Depreciation Reduces the Tax Basis of the Rental Property

Let's go back to when we were earlier saying that depreciation reduced the "cost" of the building by a certain amount each year.

While the cost is the most common method of establishing a tax basis, it's not the only consideration.

For tax purposes, there is a "basis" to each asset. That is the amount used for making tax calculations such as depreciation, or when you sell, for capital gains.

The basis, as we said, for most assets is their cost. However, with homes, that basis can vary. For example, there are substantial transaction fees when you buy a home. Most of these are added to the basis.

Or you may build an addition to the home. This is also added to the basis.

On the other hand, the basis may be reduced. Depreciation reduces the basis of the property. Here's how it works:

### Change in Basis on a Rental Due to Depreciation

| | |
|---|---|
| Original basis (cost) | $200,000 |
| Add a room | +30,000 |
| Adjusted basis | $230,000 |
| Depreciation ($7,000 annually for 10 years) | −70,000 |
| New adjusted basis | $160,000 |

Notice that although the property began with a basis of $200,000, which was its cost, that basis went up when a room was added and, more importantly here, went down when depreciation was calculated.

## What's the Importance of the Tax Basis?

The reason that we've spent some time understanding basis is because it (and the sales price) determines the capital gains (and tax) you'll have to pay when you sell.

Your capital gain on the property is the difference between the adjusted tax basis and the net sales price.

### Calculating Capital Gain

| | |
|---|---|
| Sales price (adjusted for costs of sale such as commission) | $300,000 |
| Adjusted tax basis | 160,000 |
| Capital gain (on which tax is due) | $140,000 |

Thus, to go through our rental example, you buy the property for $200,000, add a room for $30,000, which raises your basis, and then depreciate it for $70,000 which lowers the basis. When you sell, both the raising and lowering of the tax basis affects how big a capital gain you have.

**TIP** It's important to keep one's eye on the donut and not the hole. What's important here is to see that depreciation lowers the basis, which means that upon sale, there will be more capital gains (and resulting taxes).

All of which is to say that while depreciating rental real estate can produce an annual tax write-off, as noted earlier, that tax loss all comes back to haunt you as a capital gain when you sell.

Thus, in decades past, when anyone regardless of income could write off losses on real estate, what they were actually doing was converting their ordinary income to capital gains. Instead of paying a high ordinary income tax rate, over the term of their ownership they converted that income to a capital gain and paid lower capital gains tax rate.

If the case above went by rather fast, let's take it again a bit more slowly. Let's consider just one year. In that year the property sustains a loss of $7,000 (primarily from depreciation). That $7,000 was then deducted from the investor's ordinary income. That meant that the investor avoided paying ordinary income taxes (read high tax rate) on $7,000.

Now, the very next year, that property sells and it shows a $7,000 capital gain attributable to depreciation. The investor now has to pay tax on this amount. However, because it was a "capital gain" as opposed to "ordinary income," the tax rate was lower (currently 15 percent). Thus, the great tax shelter benefit of real estate was that it converted ordinary income to capital gains and reduced the tax rate.

## Doesn't That Work Now?

Not really, for two reasons. The first is that the Tax Reform Act of 1986 eliminated high-income investors from taking a deduction on their rental real estate losses. Then the Taxpayer Relief Act of 1997 reduced the capital gains rate (and added a few more wrinkles, as we'll shortly see).

To begin however, let's consider the rules with regard to taking a loss from real estate as a deduction against your ordinary income.

### Active Income

The tax law now discriminates between the types of income that we receive. Income from wages or as compensation for services is called active income. It includes commissions, consulting fees, salary, or anything similar. It's important for those involved in real estate to note that profits and losses from businesses in which you "materially participate" (except limited partnerships) are included. However, activities from real estate are specifically excluded.

### Passive Income

This is a bit trickier to define, but in general it means the profit or loss that we receive from a business activity in which we do not materially participate. This includes not only limited partnerships, but also income from any real estate that is rented out. It's important to note that real estate is specifically defined as passive.

### Portfolio Income

This is income from dividends, interest, royalties, and anything similar. We need not worry much about this here, except to note that it does not include real estate income.

Under the old law, income was income and loss was loss. You could deduct any loss on real estate from your other income. Under the current law, your personal income is considered "active" while your real estate loss is considered "passive." Since you can't deduct a passive loss from active income, you can't, in general, write off any real estate losses.

## What About the Little Guy?

We've already said that this was primarily aimed at the wealthy to eliminate a big tax shelter. But there is an advantage to be retained here for the small investor.

There is an important exception to the above rule. This exception provides a $25,000 allowance for write-offs for those with lower ordinary income. In other words, you can write off up to $25,000 in losses from real estate against your active income, provided you meet an income ceiling (plus certain other qualifications).

## Your Gross Adjusted Income Must Not Exceed $150,000

If your income is below $100,000, then you qualify for the entire $25,000 exception. If it is between $100,000 and $150,000, you lose fifty cents of the allowance for every dollar your income exceeds $100,000.

Since most small investors have incomes under $150,000 the allowance applies to them. They can deduct their losses on real estate up to the $25,000 limitation.

## What's the Other Qualification?

You'll recall that we said there was another qualification. It is that you must actively participate in the business of renting the property.

This can be tricky, after all, what does "actively participate" really mean?

Obviously, if you own the property and are the only person directly involved in handling the rental—you advertise it, rent it, handle maintenance and cleanup, collect the rent, etc.—then you materially participate.

However, there are gray zones. Generally, if you don't personally determine the rental terms, approve new tenants, sign for repairs, or approve capital improvements and the like, then you may not qualify.

The question always comes up, "What if I hire a management firm to handle the property for me?"

This is even grayer. In general, a management firm is probably okay to use as long as you continue to materially participate— determine rental terms, approve new tenants, sign for repairs or capital improvements, and the like. If you are going to use a management firm, be sure that you have your attorney check over the agreement you sign with the firm to see that it does not characterize you as not materially participating and thus prevent you from deducting any loss.

## Are There Any Other Kinks in the Rules?

On the surface, the allowance and the qualifications may seem straightforward. But they can be tricky. For example, here are some other considerations:

1. The income used to determine whether you qualify is your gross adjusted income. This means your income after you have taken some deductions, such as some

retirement plan contributions (not IRAs), alimony, moving expenses, and others.

2. The allowance does not apply to farms. If you materially participate in the running of a farm, other rules apply— see your accountant or tax attorney.

3. Those who don't qualify for taking the deduction against their active income cannot likewise take the deduction against their portfolio income. (Remember, portfolio income comes from interest, dividends, royalties, etc.)

## So When You Sell, Chances Are You Will Owe Some Capital Gains

Yes, assuming you've converted your personal residence to a rental business and don't sell for a loss. However, as noted, the capital gains tax rate has been reduced. At the present time it's a maximum of 15 percent. Hence, even if you do have to pay, it won't be a confiscatory amount.

## Is There Any Legal Way to Avoid a Tax on Your Profits from Your Rental Property?

The first method which might be used is to convert the property from an investment to a personal residence. You can remove the tenants and move in yourself, declaring the property your principal residence. After a period of time, you may then be able to sell the home and reap the benefits of the principal residence capital gains exclusion which we discussed at the beginning of this chapter.

There are certain problems with this scenario, however. The first is, how long must you reside in the property to make it your personal residence? I don't know of any hard and fast rule.

Some accountants say two years, others longer. Check with your professional tax advisor.

The second has to do with all that depreciation taken while you owned the property. Under the current rules, it is recaptured at a special rate. Thus, even though you may avoid paying taxes on most of your capital gains by using the personal property exclusion, you might still owe some taxes on the recaptured depreciation losses that you took earlier.

Yet another problem, here, is that very often the investor is not really interested in moving into the rental property. In that case, a tax-deferred exchange, as described below, might be better.

## Is There Another Way of Legally Avoiding Paying Taxes on Your Capital Gain on a Rental?

Yes, there is. You can trade your rental property for another and defer the capital gain from the old property to the new. This is technically called a Section 1031 Tax-Deferred Exchange.

**TRAP**

The 1031 tax-deferred exchange is not for novices. If you want to do one, be sure you get professional advice.

A great many investors see this as a means of multiplying their profits without paying taxes along the way. They hopscotch from property to property, increasing the value of their real estate holdings unencumbered by paying taxes for each transaction.

**TIP**

Normally, in a strict sale and then purchase of another property, you would pay taxes on your capital gain. That would leave you less equity to invest in the next property. However, by deferring that tax bill into the future, you have all your equity to put into the next property, meaning you can buy a bigger and better investment!

The rules for a tax-free exchange were greatly simplified over a decade ago by several tax cases the most famous of which is called the "Starker rule." Under Starker, you just go ahead and sell your investment property as you would otherwise. However, you have 45 days after the sale to designate a new property into which you will invest your money. And you have 180 days to close the deal on that new property. (These timelines run concurrently and are not extendable.)

Note that there are other strict conditions of the exchange which must be met. One is that you may not take cash out ("boot out") or you could endanger the tax-deferred status of the trade. If you want cash out, you must usually refinance the old property before the exchange or the new property after it.

Another condition is that only like-kind properties can be exchanged. This generally means any property held for investment or business purposes. Thus you could exchange a rental house for a commercial building.

Yet another condition is that after the exchange you must maintain the property as an investment (not move in yourself) for at least a year.

As I said, 1031 exchanges are not for novices and you should seek professional help before you run one.

## Can You Combine an Exchange and a Personal Property Exclusion?

One of the problems we noted earlier with converting an investment property into a personal property was that you may not want to reside in a property you own as an investment. If that's the case, then the answer could be simple. Just do a tax-deferred exchange of the investment property into one in which you would like to live. Maintain it for at least a year as an investment (so as not to disallow the 1031 exchange), then convert the desirable home from investment to principal residence by moving in and living there for the requisite period of time.

**TRAP**

Newer tax rules require that you own the property you convert using a 1031 tax-deferred sale as a personal residence for five years before you can claim the exclusion.

## Keep Good Records

As noted earlier, you need good record keeping. You may have to prove to the IRS that expenses that you had on your investment property were real. For example, three years earlier you had a vacancy and you spent $115 advertising to get a new tenant.

Prove it, says the IRS. So you reach into your bag of receipts and pull out an invoice from the local newspaper for $115 for advertising. Attached to it is a copy of the ad itself and your check in payment. That would be hard to dispute.

Also, keep all records if you make improvements to the property. Remember, improvements *raise* the tax basis which will later reduce the amount of capital gains you will need to pay. (The higher the tax basis, the less the capital gain.)

If you make a capital improvement, such as add a new room, keep all of the receipts. At the end of the year your accountant will be able to use them to adjust your tax basis upwards.

**TIP**

Just because you spend money improving your rental doesn't mean that you've made a capital improvement for tax purposes. Replacing a water heater, for example, is not a capital improvement, it's a repair. Adding a tile roof where there was previously a less expensive tar roof might be a capital improvement (at least the difference in price between the tar roof and the tile).

## What If You Refinance?

As strange as it may seem, refinancing your property without a sale has no immediate tax consequences. You don't report new mortgages to the IRS. You will, however, have less equity to rely upon later when you do sell and must pay capital gains taxes.

# 7 Things to Do When It Just Won't Sell

You put the home up for sale, and for whatever reason the property doesn't sell. And doesn't sell. And still doesn't sell. (Does this sound familiar?)

This can be one of life's more frustrating situations. It can lead to indigestion, difficulties at work, and even marital problems. In a difficult market it can also lead to money lost, foreclosure, and bad credit.

## What Should You Do?

The first thing that you as a seller should do when your house doesn't sell as fast as you hoped it would is to dump those fears that you have. Yes, you can sell your house. For every home, there is a buyer. You just haven't found yours yet. Ultimately, there is no house that can't be sold, unless the market is totally dead. Even in a challenging market, some houses are selling. If other houses can be sold, yours can be, too.

What you have to do is to stand back and analyze the situation. Find out what's causing the problem and take steps to correct it.

## Why Your House Isn't Selling

Generally, you can trace the problem back to one or more of seven reasons:

### The 7 Reasons Why Homes Don't Sell

1. **Price.** You're asking too much.
2. **Time.** You just haven't given it enough time.
3. **Exposure.** Not enough people know it's for sale.
4. **Market.** Sales all around you are very slow.
5. **Neighborhood.** The neighborhood's got problems.
6. **Condition.** You haven't fixed it up enough.
7. **Terms.** You aren't competing well with other sellers.

Here are things you can do:

## 1. Offer a Better Price

How can I get my price, and offer a good value to the buyer too?

The hardest thing for most sellers to accept is price realism. When you're selling, whether it be T-shirts, bananas, or houses, you're in competition with others selling the same or very similar products. If the vendor down the road is selling bananas for 67 cents a pound, how many people do you think will pay you $1.02 a pound? They'll say, "Why should I pay more? I'll go down the street and get the same bananas for less." It's the same for houses.

In order to sell, your price must be competitive. If you ask more than the market will bear, even just a thousand dollars more in a rough market, it'll take much longer to sell, if you ever do.

**TRAP**

Don't get hung up on price. A property is worth just what a buyer will pay for it and no more. The hard truth is that it makes no difference how much you paid, how much you owe, or how much you put into it. Only the market determines the price.

With this said, it's important to understand that you can indeed get a better price than your neighbor for your house *if* you can convince a buyer that you have a superior product. The reason that you're charging $1.02 for your bananas is that they are organically grown. Or they are bigger. Or they taste better. Some buyers looking for a superior product will pay your higher price.

In other words, if you can convince buyers that your house is in some way superior to seemingly comparable homes selling for less, you can get more. The difficulty is in convincing the buyers, who these days are very savvy. Remember, buyers shop neighborhood first. Thus, they already have a good idea of what your house should be worth, given its location, even before they stop by.

Nevertheless, within every neighborhood there's a price *range*. You want to be at top of the range, not at the bottom or even near the middle. What can you do to accomplish this?

You can't change the size of your house. If you have 1,500 square feet, you can't make it into 1,800. (Unless you add on, but that might mean you're overbuilding for your neighborhood and you might get only 50 cents on the dollar for what it costs to do the work.)

But you can "doll up" your house. You can make its appearance so irresistible that a buyer will perceive you have a better product and be willing to pay more for your home than for the "dog" that your neighbor down the street is selling for less. (Refer back to Chapters 1 and 2.)

## 2. Give It More Time

Remember that the amount of time that it takes to sell a home differs with each property and according to the market. Perhaps you went to a local agent and discovered that the average time to sell a home in your area was 180 days. So you assumed your home would sell within six months. Now seven months have gone by and it hasn't sold.

What happened?

Perhaps something is indeed wrong and you should check out the other causes for not selling that are listed below. But, assuming that one or more of those aren't amiss, perhaps you just have to give it more time. Remember, to sell a house you need only one buyer.

But, like fishing, you have to wait for that buyer to get hooked.

**TIP**

The newer the listing, the easier it is to sell at full price. The longer you have your home on the market, the more you'll have to drop your price to attract buyers.

**TRAP**

The average length of time for sale is just that, an "average." Remember, many houses take longer to sell and many sell faster. In some areas of the country, in a challenging market it takes longer, sometimes as much as a year, to sell.

## 3. Spread the Word Further About Your House

Lack of exposure simply means that enough buyers haven't been made aware of the fact that your home is for sale. There are several ways of tracking exposure.

1. **Count the number of buyers who come through your house.**
   Counting heads is the easiest approach. Or you can have a little sign in book at the door. If you haven't had a visit

from a buyer in several weeks, it's a bad sign. On the other hand, if buyers keep coming through and looking and there are no offers, you may have a problem with price or terms. (Reread Chapters 2 and 9.)

2. **Count the number of real estate people who come through.** Assuming you have your house listed, you should have "caravans" of agents coming through, particularly when the house first goes on the market. Whole offices of agents, who are now aware your property is listed, will come by to see it, to remember it, and to determine if they have any buyers for it. Later, individual agents will come by seeing if your house is right for a particular buyer they have.

   When agents come by, they usually leave their business card. Count the cards. If there are only a few, it could mean trouble. Agents know that they can't see all the houses for sale, so they pick out only the most likely ones. Few business cards means they may be avoiding your house. Call your agent and ask if she has been "talking up" your house at agents' meetings. Ask if there is something you can do, such as offering a bonus to the selling agent that will spark interest. (And reread Chapter 3.)

3. **Count the number of calls that you get.** If you're selling FSBO, you undoubtedly have a sign out and an ad in the paper. If you do, you're bound to get calls. If those calls don't come in, or if there are very few of them, or if the potential buyers who call are confused about what you're selling or hang up when you explain what you've got, you may have a problem. Recheck your advertising for clarity and impact. Make sure you call back everyone who rings you up. (And reread Chapter 7.)

## 4. Recheck the Market

Have you analyzed the local real estate market to see what condition it's in? You can expect a sale in a fairly short time in a hot or stable market. But if the market's declining or in recession, it may take a very long time to sell.

If your reanalyze the market and are convinced that it's at least stable, then look closely at other factors, particularly the condition of your home, the neighborhood, and the price.

On the other hand, if you discover that the market is weak, then some reevaluation regarding the sale may be in order. In a cold market you may not be able to sell your home for a reasonable price—regardless of how much time you spend trying—until the market turns around. In a very bad market, there simply are very few buyers at all.

What can you do in a weak market to help get a sale? Consider seller financing (Chapter 9) or using incentives (Chapter 10). In fact, reread most of the chapters in this book, as they will give you great ideas for moving your home in a down market. You could always rent or lease option your home.

It may take longer to sell in a challenging market, but any home can eventually be sold. Even yours!

## 5. Work on Your Neighborhood Influence

Everyone knows that the three biggest considerations when buying real estate are location, location, and location. However, you may think that your neighborhood is okay, only to realize that others don't feel the same way. For example, your neighborhood may have deteriorated during the time you've lived there and you haven't really noticed. Or a big lumber mill a mile away never bothered you, but it turns off potential buyers.

You'll know if the neighborhood is the problem because people will tell you. Agents will tell you. Home hunters who stop by will tell you (if you ask). Even some of your neighbors will tell you.

If it turns out that your house isn't selling because it's in a bad location, what can you do about it? The best thing you could have done was to have bought in a better neighborhood. (Remember this for next time.) But, now you're stuck. As sellers, we can't offer buyers a better neighborhood. Or can we?

Obviously, you can't change a neighborhood, at least not overnight. But you can do some things to improve the neighbors around you. And you can sometimes expand a potential buyer's perspective on the true quality of your area.

A few years ago a friend of mine had a home he was trying to sell in a rather rundown area. To make things worse, neighbors across the street were in the habit of working on their cars on their front lawn.

Potential buyers would drive up to my friend's house, only to see the mess across the street. Most wouldn't even stop—they'd just drive on.

After many months, my friend sold his property for far less than he had in it. He virtually "gave it away." The new owner was an investor. She immediately put the house back up for sale. She was planning a flip.

Then she went across the street to the bad neighbors, knocked on the door, and asked a favor.

She said, "I'm trying to teach my son responsibility and how to do a good job. I wonder if you'd mind if he came over and mowed your lawn? It'll be a good experience for him." The neighbor was astonished and looked across the street to a perfectly manicured lawn. "Sure," the neighbor said. "Why not?"

"Fine" she said, "How soon can you move the car?"

The neighbor was taken aback. But something clicked. Maybe it was embarrassment of the appearance of the home. Soon after, the car(s) were moved into the garage and every week her son went over to mow the lawn, trim the bushes, sometimes even to water. The neighbor felt he was getting a good deal. And the investor never mentioned the $25 a week she was paying her son.

Others in the neighborhood, who were relieved to see the mess cleaned up, began complimenting the bad neighbor, who felt even better about that. Soon other neighbors also cleaned up their front yards.

She resold that home within a few months for a substantial profit. Nothing will pop the price of a home up faster than neighborhood improvement.

**Improve the Perception of the Neighborhood.**   Even if you do improve the look of homes on your street, you can't give your home a Beverly Hills address unless it's in Beverly Hills—or can you?

I once had a home that was in a modest area, but near the border of a highly desired area. When I advertised my property, did I say I was in the modest area? Or did my ad say "next to" the more desired neighborhood?

Further, when potential buyers stop by and are wary of the area, you can make an effort to demonstrate that your neighborhood is greatly underrated. You can point out that few people realize that you have a park nearby, are close to shopping, have great access to freeways, have green belts, or that your school tests scores are going up. In other words, your neighborhood actually is far better than commonly perceived.

Furthermore, you can explain that people are just now discovering the true value of your neighborhood. Why, within a year or two, yours could be among the most desired in the county, perhaps the state. The purchaser of your home will be getting in cheap, before people in general realize how much more desirable an area it really is and prices go up.

Will buyers believe it? If it's close enough to the truth, many will.

For most people, the perception is more important than the reality, the sizzle more mouthwatering than the steak. As long as buyers perceive you're in a desirable neighborhood, it doesn't matter how good or bad your area really is.

## 6. Rethink Your Home's Condition

For now let's assume that there's nothing drastically wrong with your home (no holes in the walls, no broken floors, no caved in roof, and so on). If you haven't already done them, here are the four most important, inexpensive, and quick cosmetic improvements you can make to get a quicker sale:

### Four Best Improvements to Make to Get a Quick Sale

1. **Work on that driveway.** A driveway takes up an enormous amount of the front of your home. It's what people usually first see when they drive up. It's often what they first walk on. If it's cracked, broken, or even dirty, it sets the tone for the rest of the house.

   Wash your driveway. (Use one of the many commercial cleaners available to get rid of stains.) If it's badly cracked and it's a tar driveway, have it resurfaced. It costs only a few hundred dollars. If the driveway is cement and it's cracked, have the cracked area cut out and replaced. Often you can replace a few sections for a fraction of what it will cost for an entirely new cement driveway.

2. **Manicure the lawn and shrubs.** Again, first impressions are critical. You want the lawn to look like a carpet, the shrubs to have not a branch out of place. Get lots of green showing, water heavily for a month or more before you put the place up for sale, plant flowers—you get the idea.

3. **Paint the front.** No, it's not expensive to paint the front of your house. It's expensive to paint your whole house, but not just the front. Most people can do it themselves. Use high-quality paint and a complementary color on the trim. Most importantly, repaint that front door. The first physical contact a potential buyer makes with your house is the front door.

4. **Get rid of your clutter.** The biggest inside mistake that most sellers make is to confuse a "lived in" look with a selling look.

   Buyers like spaciousness. They want to be able to imagine how their furniture will look in your home. Never mind that once they move in, it will be just as cluttered as your home is for you. You have to give them every opportunity to help them "see" themselves in your house.

   Think of models for new homes that you may have seen. Did you notice that in the most charming models, the furniture was sparse, barely enough to live in, probably less than you'd find in the average hotel room?

   You want to create an atmosphere of "negative space," where the rooms in your house cry out to be filled with more furniture—the buyer's furniture!

   It doesn't matter what you do with most of your own furniture—put it in storage, leave it at a relative's or friend's house, sell it, burn it! Just get rid of it to help sell your home.

   Also, reread Chapter 4.

### 7. Offer Better Terms

What we all want is a buyer to come in and give us our price, *in cash.*

The trouble is that these days, fewer buyers have cash. Indeed, according to government statistics, we're a nation of consumers, not savers. Exclusive of retirement, less than 30 percent of the population has any sizable amount of cash savings at all, certainly not enough to cover a large down payment and closing costs when it comes time to buy a home.

Therefore, you can significantly increase the number of potential buyers for your home (and beat the competition) by offering to help them with the financing.

> Any time a buyer sees "seller financing" advertised or in a listing, it's a come-on. **TIP** Immediately the buyer is more inclined to look at the property and to find a way to make an offer.

What is seller financing? Usually it means that you trade cash for paper (see Chapter 9). Instead of getting all cash back yourself, you carry back a second mortgage.

You want to sell faster and for more money? Offer the buyer financing. It makes your house much more desirable than those of other sellers who can't or won't. And you'll increase the potential number of buyers who will be interested.

## The Bottom Line

These then are the seven best and quickest things you can do to facilitate a sale of your home when it's stuck on the market. Oh, here are a couple of extras:

- **Don't let your listing get "stale."** Agents and buyers tend to stop looking at listings that have been on the market for months. Take your house off for a while then relist. Yes, the computerized listing services will note that your home was previously listed. But many buyers will not know to check and will think yours is a new listing.

- **Be more flexible.** After you sell, you plan to move out anyway, don't you? So, if buyers come along who say that they'll take your place and close escrow in three weeks, provided you can move out by then, do it! You can always temporarily store your furniture and move into an apartment. But the important thing is that your house will be sold. On the other hand, some buyers want a long escrow. They may not want to take possession until 90 or 120 days or more. They're waiting for their own home to close, or for money to arrive from an inheritance, or they don't want to change schools in midyear. The point is they want you to wait. Do it. The more flexible you can be, the better your chances of selling.

Work on delivering all seven, plus the two bonus tips in this chapter. Remember, we live in a highly competitive society, and nowhere is that competition tougher than in real estate. If you want to get your house sold, you need an edge. That edge comes from going out of your way to make your property more salable.

There's a buyer for every house. The only real question is: how long will it take that person to find your house?

# Index

# About the Author

ROBERT IRWIN is one of America's foremost experts in every area of real estate. He is the author of McGraw-Hill's bestselling Tips and Traps series, as well as *The Home Buyer's Checklist, How to Get Started in Real Estate Investing,* and *How to Buy a Home When You Can't Afford It.* His books have sold more than one million copies. Visit his Web site at www.robertirwin.com.